A Love Worth Waiting For:

Mariangeli Morauske

Copyright © 2025 by Mariángeli Morauske.

Mariángeli Morauske, MD, MACP., MAPM., Ch., affirms the moral right to be identified as the author of this work.

Edited by and Graphic design and composition: Mariangeli Morauske

Top image: Artificial Intelligent. It does not correspond to real people.

Printed in the United States of America. All rights reserved. Imprint: Published independently.

No part of this book may be reproduced, stored in a retrieval system, or transmitted in any form or by any means, electronic, mechanical, photocopying, recording, scanning, or otherwise, without the prior written permission of the author, except for short quotations used in critical reviews or articles. Permission can be requested by contacting the author by email at endtimessequence@aol.com.

Unless otherwise indicated, all quotations from Sacred Scripture are taken from the 1960 King James Version.

"The biblical quotations are taken from The Holy Bible, New International® Version (NIV®), Copyright © 1973, 1978, 1984, 2011 by Biblica, Inc. Used under the fair use provisions of U.S. copyright law. All rights reserved worldwide."

Ellen G. White's quotes are from the online collection of her writings available on www.egwwritings.org. Copyright © 2025 by Ellen G. White Estate, Inc. Used under the fair use provisions of U.S. copyright law. All rights reserved.

ISBN: 979-8-89860-255-0 Cobertura Dura

A Love Worth Waiting: Happily Ever After

Table of Contents

Dedication vii

A Word to the Reader ix

Chapter 1   Dating: A Sacred Prelude or a Dangerous Game? 1

   A Walk Among Roses and Thorns 1

   10 Signs You Are Dating God's Way 3

Chapter 2 Broken Before the Vows: Why Good Intentions Fail Without God's Foundation 15

   Why Good Intentions Fail 17

   God's Way: Slow. Sacred. Spirit-Led 19

Chapter 3 From "I Do" to "I Can't": The Real Reasons Love Fails 25

   5 Silent Killers of Marriage 27

   God's Blueprint for Love That Lasts 30

Chapter 4   The Cracks Before the Covenant: Unhealed Wounds in Sacred Unions 35

   Hidden Cracks That Break a Covenant 36

   How to Repair the Cracks Before They Collapse the Home 41

A Love Worth Waiting: Happily Ever After

Chapter 5 Building on Sand: Why Passion Without Principle Destroys Marriage..43

    5 Warning Signs You're Building on Sand 44

Chapter 6 The Silent Erosion: How Little Things Undermine a Marriage Before It Starts..57

    The Little Foxes That Spoil Great Love 58

    Restoring the Foundation — One Brick at a Time 63

Chapter 7 When Red Flags Wear White Dresses: Discernment Before You Say 'I Do' 69

    7 Red Flags the Holy Spirit Wants You to See 70

Chapter 8 Soul Ties and Sacred Bonds: Emotional Connections that Heal or Harm 77

    Signs of an Unhealthy Soul Tie...78

    A Chain Broken by Christ 82

Chapter 9 The Art of Waiting: How God Prepares Hearts for Holy Love" 95

    What Happens in the Waiting?...96

    God Is Not Late — He's Precise..98

A Love Worth Waiting: Happily Ever After

Chapter 10   True Love Waits: Purity, Power, and the Purpose of Saving Yourself 107

   Why Purity Still Matters..108

   How to Guard Your Purity (or Begin Again) 110

Chapter 11   God-Written Love Stories: What Happens When You Let Him Choose..117

   5 Signs of a God-Written Love Story 119

   When God Chooses, He Also Sustains.................................123

Chapter 12   Before You Say Yes: Questions You Must Ask Before You Marry..127

   10 Questions to Ask Before You Say Yes 128

Chapter 13   Love After Yes: What to Expect and How to Prepare for Engagement..135

   7 Things to Expect During Engagement — and How to Prepare 136

Chapter 14   Marriage on Mission: What Happens When Two Become One in Christ..145

   5 Truths About Kingdom Marriages 146

Chapter 15   The First Year: How to Build Without Breaking 155

   What to Expect in the First Year (And How to Build Right)..156

A Love Worth Waiting: Happily Ever After

Chapter 16   Crisis-Proofing Your Covenant: How to Stand When the Storm Hits..167

   7 Crises That Can Shake a Marriage.....................................168

   How to Crisis-Proof Your Covenant 173

   3 Covenantal Promises for the Storm 176

Chapter 17   When Love Is Hard: Grace for Marriages in Survival Mode 179

   Signs Your Marriage May Be in Survival Mode..................181

   What to Do When Love Feels Hard......................................185

   What Grace Looks Like in Marriage.....................................189

Chapter 18   When You're Married to Someone Who Doesn't Share Your Faith 195

   What It Means to Be Unequally Yoked 196

   How to Love Someone Who Doesn't Share Your Faith.......200

   What About the Children? 205

   Practical Ways to Nurture Spiritual Growth 206

Chapter 19   God in the Mundane: Finding Heaven in Dishes, Laundry, and Bills..211

   Where Heaven Meets the Everyday 212

   How to Invite God into the Everyday 217

Chapter 20   The Prayer-Filled Home: Building an Atmosphere Where the Spirit Dwells 223
   Why Prayer Changes the Atmosphere 224
   5 Habits of a Prayer-Filled Home 228

Chapter 21 Leaving a Legacy: Love That Echoes into Eternity 233
   The Power of a Godly Legacy 234
   How to Build a Marriage That Echoes Beyond You 238

Chapter 22   Heaven at Home: A Final Charge for Youth in Love 245
   What Does Heaven at Home Look Like? 246

Premarital Inventory 254
Bibliography 255

A Love Worth Waiting: Happily Ever After

Dedication

To my precious Leilani and Josiah,

You both, are the melody in my heart, the sunlight in my days, and the steady beat that carries me through life's symphony.

Leilani, my radiant flower, your grace, and strength remind me every day that beauty blooms even in the most unexpected places. Your kind spirit and inquisitive mind are a testament to how deeply the world is blessed to have you in it. **Josiah,** my courageous dreamer, you are my anchor and my adventurer. Your laughter is the sweetest music, and your endless curiosity ignites a spark in everyone around you.

Every moment I spend with you both, I see a reflection of God's perfect love—a love that teaches patience, fills us with joy, and calls us to be the best versions of ourselves. You have taught me lessons no book or classroom ever could. From the twinkles in your eyes to the way you trust so freely, you inspire me to see life through a lens of hope and wonder.

This is only a whisper of what my heart holds for you both. You guys are my legacy, my joy, and my greatest treasures. With every breath I take and every prayer I whisper, know that you are deeply loved beyond measure, not just by me, but by the One who created you so perfectly. - Mom.

A Love Worth Waiting: Happily Ever After

A Word to the Reader

A Living and Evolving Journey

Every book has a story behind its story — one that begins long before the first word is written and continues long after the last page is turned. This book is no exception. It was not simply written; it was lived, wept over, prayed through, and born from the depths of personal experience, spiritual conviction, and a relentless desire to share truths that can transform.

As you begin to turn these pages, I want to extend a sincere invitation: walk with me — not just through the text, but through the journey that birthed it. What you are about to read is more than a manuscript; it is a living testimony. It is a tapestry woven with insights, imperfections, clarity, and questions. It reflects what I have seen, learned, and come to believe up to this point in my journey. But it is not the final word.

This is a living and evolving book.

Errors and Corrections

Although I have poured over these words with great care, I am fully aware that some mistakes may remain. Whether grammatical, typographical, or even interpretive, I acknowledge the possibility of human error. If you notice something that needs to be corrected, I welcome your grace and your voice. Please feel free to email me at **endtimessequence@aol.com**. I will gladly make necessary corrections in future editions and, with your permission, honor your contribution by giving you credit. Your help enriches the message for future readers.

A Growing Understanding

What you will read here is the fruit of my present understanding — sincere and thoughtful, but not final. My interpretation of spiritual truths is progressive. Like any student of life and faith, I am constantly growing, always listening, and open to receiving more light. As God teaches me through His Word, through people, and through experience, some insights may deepen or shift. This book, therefore, stands as a snapshot of where I am now — grateful for how far I've come, and aware that the journey is still unfolding.

I invite you to read not just with your mind, but with your heart. To reflect, wrestle, question, and apply. This book is meant to speak to the soul, to stir the spirit, and to build something beautiful in the sacred space of home and family. Your reading is not the end of this work, but part of its very purpose.

So, thank you. Thank you for being here. Thank you for giving these pages a place in your life. And thank you for being part of something that is still growing, still reaching, still becoming.

Welcome to this journey. May it be as life-giving for you to read as it was for me to write.

With gratitude, Mariangeli **Morauske**

Chapter 1
Dating: A Sacred Prelude or a Dangerous Game?

"Can two walk together, except they be agreed?" - Amos 3:3

A Walk Among Roses and Thorns

There is a season in life that comes with butterflies in the stomach, handwritten notes, stolen glances, and secret prayers whispered beneath the stars. It's the time when a heart begins to yearn for companionship — and that season is dating.

For many, dating is painted in hues of romance, poetry, and passion. It promises joy, closeness, and discovery. Yet for others, it becomes a winding road filled with confusion, tears, and scars. Some begin with dreams of "forever" and end in emotional ruins. Why?

Because the world has lost the sacred meaning of what it means to truly love — and more importantly, to prepare for it.

Love or Infatuation?

In our modern world, dating often begins too soon, moves too fast, and dives too deep — emotionally, physically, and spiritually — without asking the most important questions.

Dating, in God's plan, is not about emotional games or passing time. It is a sacred prelude, a journey of discernment. A time to *prepare* for the most important human covenant: marriage.

Ellen G. White warned long ago that if those who are contemplating marriage would not have miserable, unhappy reflections after marriage, they must make it a subject of serious, earnest reflection now.

Too many treat dating like a game, not a sacred mission. Feelings become gods. Emotions lead, not reason. And often, God's voice is drowned out by the thrill of the chase.

Dating: God's Purpose

In the divine blueprint, dating is not meant to *entertain the heart*, but to *prepare it for covenant love*. It is a window — not a destination. A time of prayerful observation, not sensual indulgence.

"Whoso findeth a wife findeth a good thing, and obtaineth favour of the Lord." - Proverbs 18:22

This implies search, intention, prayer, and divine favor. Not casual wandering from hand to hand.

Proceed with Caution

A Love Worth Waiting: Hapily Ever After

Marriage is a forever covenant — a binding oath between three: man, woman, and God. Therefore, dating should never be entered into lightly.

Ellen White speaks solemnly: "Better, far better, break the engagement before marriage than separate afterward, as many do." – *The Adventist Home*, p. 48

If there are red flags during dating, if there is pain, control, manipulation, spiritual unequally yoked paths — don't assume marriage will heal the wound. It won't. It will deepen it.

10 Signs You Are Dating God's Way

Here is an expanded, in-depth exploration of the 10 signs that reveal you are dating God's way. Each sign is not simply a checklist—it is a pathway to a relationship that reflects God's heart. As you read, may you see how seeking divine guidance, drawing on biblical wisdom, and embracing accountability can transform your relationship into a ministry of love and purpose.

1. You Both Seek God First — Not Each Other

When a relationship is rooted in a mutual pursuit of God, it lays the groundwork for a love built on a sacred foundation. This approach prioritizes seeking His presence and guidance together rather than focusing solely on individual needs or romantic feelings.

A Love Worth Waiting: Hapily Ever After

Through shared prayer, the study of Scripture, and a unified desire to fulfill God's purpose in your lives, you both align your hearts with His will. As the King James Bible beautifully states in Matthew 6:33,

"But seek ye first the kingdom of God, and his righteousness; and all these things shall be added unto you."

When both heart and mind are aligned in worship and obedience, your union becomes less about filling a void and more about reflecting divine love. For example, imagine you're deciding on a future home together. Instead of making choices based solely on personal tastes or fleeting trends, you set aside time to pray and seek God's vision. This practice unites your hearts in purpose and deepens the trust in the path He has laid before you.

2. Boundaries Are Respected, Not Constantly Tested

Healthy boundaries are like the fences that protect a fertile garden; they preserve the integrity of what God has begun in you. In a relationship that honors God, both partners agree on what is appropriate—physical, emotional, and spiritual—and they intentionally cultivate self-discipline. The Bible warns in *1 Corinthians 6:18*:

A Love Worth Waiting: Hapily Ever After

"Flee fornication. Every sin that a man doeth is without the body; but he that committeth fornication sinneth against his own body."

Ellen G. White also teaches that self-control is a safeguard against the erosion of one's character. Consider a couple who openly discusses their limitations and agrees to postpone physical expressions of love until marriage. This choice not only honors God's design but also builds trust and mutual respect, ensuring that both individuals feel safe, valued, and understood.

3. You Pray Together Before Making Decisions

Prayer is the intimate conversation with God that unites your spirits and clarifies your vision. When you pause as a couple to seek divine guidance on every major decision—whether it be about finances, career moves, or family matters—it becomes a testament to your shared faith. As *1 Thessalonians 5:17* urges us: "Pray without ceasing."

Ellen G. White once observed, "When two hearts are united in prayer, the works of the spirit empower them to overcome even the gravest difficulties." Imagine a scenario where a career opportunity arises that could pull you apart geographically. Instead of succumbing to anxiety or making a hasty decision, you come together in prayer, asking God for clarity. The peace that follows isn't just about resolving the decision—it becomes a cornerstone of your relationship, affirming that your lives are deeply intertwined with His will.

4. Your Parents and Spiritual Mentors Are Involved

A relationship that is truly guided by God welcomes counsel from those who have walked the path before and know His ways well. Involving parents and spiritual mentors brings in wisdom, accountability, and support. The Scriptures remind us in *Proverbs 11:14*: "Where no counsel is, the people fall: but in the multitude of counsellors there is safety."

For example, a young couple facing a challenging decision might turn to a trusted church elder or their parents for advice. This validates their choices with godly insight and weaves the relationship into a broader tapestry of faith and community. Ellen G. White emphasized that "When advice is sought from godly counselors, the clear light of truth illuminates the darkest of dilemmas." The involvement of mentors cements a tradition of humility and collective discernment.

5. Your Communication Is Open and Honest

Transparency in communication is the heartbeat of any healthy relationship. When you speak your truth with love and listen with empathy, you create a space where both hearts can flourish. The Bible advises in *Proverbs*

A Love Worth Waiting: Hapily Ever After

15:1: "A soft answer turneth away wrath: but grievous words stir up anger."

Ellen G. White also stressed that cultivating honesty nurtures the soul and builds character. Consider a time when you faced disappointment or misunderstanding. Being able to share your feelings honestly, without fear of judgment or hidden agendas, allows both partners to address issues head-on and grow together. This kind of forthright communication not only prevents resentment but also enhances intimacy and mutual respect.

6. You're Developing Friendship, Not Just Physical Closeness

A Christ-centered relationship is rooted in deep, abiding friendship rather than merely physical attraction. True companionship is reflective of God's love—a love that is patient, kind, and enduring. *Proverbs 17:17* illustrates this beautifully: "A friend loveth at all times, and a brother is born for adversity."

Building a relationship on friendship means engaging in shared hobbies, serving together in your church, or simply spending quality time discussing your dreams and struggles. One couple might find that volunteering at a local shelter provides community service and deepens their connection by aligning their hearts with God's compassion. As Ellen G. White noted, "The foundation of a lasting relationship is laid in the friendship that bonds two souls in true fellowship."

7. You're Not Hiding Your Relationship

When a relationship is grounded in honesty and godliness, there is nothing to hide. Openly sharing your partnership with friends, family, and your church community is a powerful statement of faith and integrity. *Matthew 5:16* encourages us to live transparently: "Let your light so shine before men, that they may see your good works, and glorify your Father which is in heaven."

An example of this might be a couple who proudly attends church together, participates in community events, and even shares their journey on social media — not for vanity, but to inspire others. Such openness not only increases accountability but also invites encouragement and prayer from a supportive community. It signals that your relationship is a sacred trust, blessed and visible before God.

8. You're Growing Spiritually — Not Compromising Convictions

A relationship that honors God is not a compromise of your values but a catalyst for spiritual growth. When the core of your union is built on unyielding conviction, both partners commit to a life of ongoing transformation. The apostle Paul exhorts in *Romans 12:2*:

"And be not conformed to this world: but be ye transformed by the renewing of your mind, that ye may prove what is that good, and acceptable, and perfect, will of God."

Ellen G. White reminds us that "To stand in the light of the truth, even when it is difficult, is the true test of character." An example of this might be a moment when one partner feels tempted to stray from their principles due to societal pressures. Instead of yielding, the couple chooses reinforcements in prayer, Bible study, and honest dialogue, thereby strengthening their resolve. In doing so, they honor their convictions and inspire one another to grow closer to God.

9. You Trust Each Other When Apart

Trust is the unseen thread that holds the fabric of a relationship together. When you can be apart — perhaps due to work, study, or service — yet remain confident in the bond you share, you demonstrate a profound trust in God's design. As written in *Romans 12:9*:

"Let love be without dissimulation. Abhor that which is evil; cleave to that which is good."

For instance, consider a scenario where one partner travels for a conference or ministry work.

A Love Worth Waiting: Hapily Ever After

Communication and mutual encouragement during this time reinforce your trust and independence, reminding you that the relationship is secure regardless of physical distance. This trust, rooted in faith and the understanding that God is the ultimate keeper of your hearts, fortifies the union and allows personal growth while sustaining intimacy.

10. You Could Walk Away with Peace if God Asked You To

Perhaps the most profound indicator of a God-honoring relationship is the readiness to obey God—even when it means parting ways. This is not a sign of weakness but of true strength and deep faith. It signifies that your commitment is not to the fleeting comforts of human affirmation but to the eternal truth of God's calling. While the Bible does not provide a direct verse on this aspect, the principle is woven throughout Scripture, reminding us that divine guidance must always take precedence over personal desire. In the words of Ellen G. White, "When God directs you to forsake that which you cherish, be not dismayed; the pathway He opens is the way to perfect peace."

Imagine facing a crossroads where continuing the relationship might mean compromising on core beliefs; if, through prayer and reflection, both partners discern that separation is God's will, then doing so with a peaceful heart becomes the highest act of obedience. In this way, you learn that true love honors God above all else—even when that means letting go.

Dating God's way is not a checklist of rules but a lifestyle that cultivates spiritual intimacy, accountability, and unwavering faith. It challenges both partners to rise above transient attractions and to pursue a relationship marked by divine order and eternal purpose. As *Romans 12:9* (KJV) advises, "Let love be without dissimulation," and as Ellen G. White reminds us in her writings, true relationships shine with the light of God's love because they are built on obedience, prayer, and a willingness to honor Him above all else.

Embrace these signs as stepping stones to a relationship that becomes not only a union of hearts but also a vibrant testimony of God's transforming grace.

May this deeper reflection inspire you to nurture a relationship that is both passionate and purposeful—a true reflection of God's way.

A Prayer for the Dating Season

Lord, teach me to wait on Your timing. Help me not to rush ahead of Your plan or be led by my emotions. Let my heart be guarded and guided by You. And if I am to love someone, may I love them in You, for You, and with You. Amen.

A Love Worth Waiting: Hapily Ever After

REFLECTION QUESTIONS

1. Have I made God the center of my dating life?

2. Am I dating with purpose – or simply to feel loved?

3. Would I want someone to date my son or daughter the way I date?

4. What would Jesus say about the relationship I'm in right now?

A Love Worth Waiting: Hapily Ever After

📝 JOURNAL PROMPT

"Spend some quiet time reflecting on your current approach to relationships and dating. Write a letter to God, inviting Him to be fully present in this area of your life. As you write, consider the following:

- What changes might occur if I truly placed God at the center of my dating life?

- How can I align my intentions with a greater purpose, rather than seeking validation or temporary affection?

- Imagine my son or daughter observing my dating choices—what lesson would they take away, and how would I feel about it?

- Reflect on Jesus' perspective—what might He lovingly advise or commend about the choices I've made?"

Let this letter be a space for honesty, growth, and spiritual insight.

A Love Worth Waiting: Hapily Ever After

Chapter 2
Broken Before the Vows: Why Good Intentions Fail Without God's Foundation

"Except the Lord build the house, they labour in vain that build it: except the Lord keep the city, the watchman waketh but in vain." – Psalm 127:1

When the Honeymoon Ends in Silence

They danced under fairy lights. Her white dress sparkled with every step. He whispered vows with trembling hands, his voice thick with emotion. The guests cheered. The cake was cut. The kiss sealed it all.

But six months later, they slept in separate rooms.

Married. Still young. Still beautiful. But deeply, heartbreakingly alone.

What happened?

It wasn't abuse. It wasn't infidelity. It wasn't even a great fight. It was something more insidious — **neglect of foundation**. They built a house of dreams, but on no bedrock. It looked strong on the outside — Instagram-worthy. But storms came. And the cracks deepened. Silence grew louder than laughter. And love — or what they had mistaken for it — dissolved into numb cohabitation.

A Love Worth Waiting: Hapily Ever After

"The Lord wants His children to have homes of peace, of joy, and of prayer. But many build upon the sand of impulse and emotion. Then they wonder why everything is falling apart." – Adapted from Ellen G. White, The Adventist Home, p. 28

This is not just one story. It is thousands. Good people. Good intentions. But a house built without God — and therefore, destined to fall.

Story: Carla & Luis — "I Never Saw It Coming"

Carla was a vibrant youth leader, always the first to arrive and the last to leave. Luis was charming, kind, and passionate about missions. Their courtship seemed perfect — two "church kids," always surrounded by friends and smiles.

They didn't argue. They led worship together. Everyone said they were "meant to be." But deep down, Carla had doubts. Luis didn't like to pray together — "too awkward," he said. He wasn't interested in Bible study, didn't open up emotionally, and didn't talk about long-term plans.

But Carla told herself, "He's a good man. He'll grow. Maybe after we're married…"

He didn't. Two years into marriage, Carla sat across from a counselor, tears rolling down her cheeks. "He never wanted God," she said. "I thought our love

A Love Worth Waiting: Hapily Ever After

would carry us. I never realized I was carrying it alone."

Why Good Intentions Fail

Most couples don't marry intending to hurt each other. They don't walk down the aisle thinking, *"Let's divorce in five years."* But many do. And the saddest part? The warning signs were often there — they were just ignored.

Let's unpack the silent saboteurs of relationships that start with fire and end with ash.

1. Lack of Premarital Discernment

Marriage is not a spiritual Band-Aid. It does not heal dating dysfunctions. It magnifies them.

"Take time to weigh the character and habits of the one with whom you think to unite your life destiny. If you are not prepared to bear their burden of soul for eternity, you are not prepared to marry them." - Messages to Young People, p. 460

Too often, people confuse chemistry with compatibility, or time invested with commitment. They say, *"But we've been together for years."* Yet years of chaos do not equal a lifetime of joy. Clarity is more important than history.

2. Romantic Expectations, Unrealistic Realities

Many thinks love means *never feeling lonely, never disagreeing,* or *always feeling butterflies.* But these expectations are myths.

"The heart is deceitful above all things..." - Jeremiah 17:9

Real love lives in the everyday — in the dishes, in the laundry, in the patience to listen even when tired. When expectations are built on fantasy, reality feels like failure.

3. Unhealed Childhood Wounds

The traumas of childhood don't disappear when you say "I do." If you never learned to communicate, to trust, to process anger — marriage will not teach you. It will expose you.

"The stronghold of the home is character. Where this is neglected, everything crumbles. What we bring into marriage is not just our love, but our scars." - The Adventist Home, p. 360

4. Spiritual Unequally Yoked Relationships

Being "spiritually attractive" is not enough. Being on fire for God matters more than being in love with someone religious.

A Love Worth Waiting: Hapily Ever After

"Be ye not unequally yoked together with unbelievers…" – 2 Corinthians 6:14

When one is trying to grow spiritually and the other is spiritually asleep — or worse, spiritually resistant — they will walk in opposite directions. Unity cannot flourish in opposition.

5. Rushing Without Knowing

Fast dating is often emotional desperation disguised as romance. The longer the wait, the clearer the truth.

"Love is a plant of heavenly origin. It must be fostered carefully, or it will perish." – The Adventist Home, p. 50

A garden must be watered, observed, tested, pruned — not thrown into a storm before its roots are ready. Likewise, a relationship must grow through seasons: laughter, hardship, confrontation, silence. If it cannot stand the seasons of courtship, it cannot survive the winters of marriage.

God's Way: Slow. Sacred. Spirit-Led.

Below is an expanded, in-depth exploration of **God's Way: Slow. Sacred. Spirit-Led.** This reflection invites you to understand that God does not rush what He treasures. His timing is thoughtful, measured, and filled with sacred purpose. As you seek to build a relationship that honors Him, consider these insights and questions to guide your journey.

God's Timing Is Deliberate and Divine

God's way is never hurried. When He brought Eve to Adam, the process was not instantaneous—it was a measured, deliberate act of divine artistry. This sacred timing reflects God's care in crafting relationships that mirror His perfect love. Just as a master artist takes time to complete every stroke, God ensures that every detail of your life and future relationships is orchestrated with intentionality.

Proverbs 19:14 reminds us, **"A prudent wife is from the Lord."** This verse underscores that wisdom in choosing a spouse comes from God. It tells us that a godly partner is not found by impulsive decisions but through a process marked by patience and discernment.

Prudence: Intentional, Not Passive

Prudence is more than cautious behavior—it is about living intentionally. When you walk with God, you naturally learn to move in the Spirit, making every decision with thoughtful care. In your search for a life partner, it isn't enough to simply find someone to "do life" with. Instead, you actively seek a relationship in which every moment is touched by divine purpose.

Ask yourself:

- Can I worship beside this person in spirit and in truth?

- Can I raise children in the fear of God with them?

- Can I grow old and still pray with them?

These questions help you evaluate whether a potential relationship is built on a foundation that honors God. They remind you that a marriage modeled on His ways is not only about companionship but also about a shared mission—to grow together in faith and to reflect the love and character of Christ.

Living Out a Spirit-Led, Sacred Love

Imagine a couple who deliberately sets aside time not only to enjoy each other's company but also to seek God together. They might attend church regularly, support one another's spiritual growth through Bible study and prayer, and serve together in their community. Their relationship isn't rushed—it is cultivated slowly, with each moment steeped in reverence for God's timing and truth. This is the essence of a sacred, spirit-led union.

A Love Worth Waiting: Hapily Ever After

When you allow God to guide your heart and your decisions, you develop a relationship that reflects Christ's love for His Church. The journey might be slow, but it is filled with moments of deep connection, growth, and Thanksgiving.

God's way is slow, sacred, and spirit-led. He does not rush what He values. Instead, He leads us with divine intentionality—a process that transforms ordinary relationships into extraordinary covenants. As you seek a partner, remember to look beyond mere convenience and fleeting attraction. Inquire of God's wisdom with questions that probe the depth of spiritual compatibility, ensuring that your relationship becomes a living testimony of worship, intentional growth, and the enduring presence of God in every season of life.

May this reflection guide you in seeking and cultivating a relationship that is not only loving but also profoundly aligned with God's slow, sacred, and spirit-led plan.

Prayer for Wisdom in Love

Father, I want more than feelings. I want wisdom. I want a love that is deep, tested, sanctified, and approved by You. Show me what I must heal. Show me what I must walk away from. Show me who I can grow holy with. Make me ready for the kind of love that reflects You. Amen.

A Love Worth Waiting: Hapily Ever After

REFLECTION QUESTIONS

1. Have I ignored red flags in the name of love or time invested?

2. What emotional or spiritual gaps have I overlooked in my relationship?

3. How has my family of origin shaped how I see marriage?

4. What does God's Word say about the relationship I am pursuing?

🙏 JOURNAL PROMPT

Describe your dream marriage. Now, list the character traits required to sustain that marriage. Ask yourself: am I becoming that kind of person? Is my partner?

A Love Worth Waiting: Hapily Ever After

Chapter 3
From "I Do" to "I Can't": The Real Reasons Love Fails

"The heart is deceitful above all things, and desperately wicked: who can know it?" – Jeremiah 17:9, KJV

What They Didn't See Coming

They said "I do" with trembling smiles. The church was full. The cake was sweet. The vows were sacred. And yet, three years later, what they now say is "I can't." I can't communicate. I can't keep forgiving. I can't keep hoping. I can't go on.

No one walks into marriage planning to walk out. But many do. Not because they didn't love — but because they didn't understand what love really means. Some never learned how to stay when staying got hard. Others never healed from wounds they carried into the marriage like ticking emotional bombs.

So they go from covenant to collapse — whispering, "I thought love would be enough."

"Many marriages are not formed from principle. The impulse of passion, the fascination of outward appearance, blinds reason and turns the heart away from God's plan. And when the emotion fades, the soul

A Love Worth Waiting: Hapily Ever After

is left hungry." — (Ellen G. White, *Messages to Young People*, p. 452)

Story: When Love Isn't Built to Last

Mariana and Julio met in a church choir. She was quiet and thoughtful; he was charming and full of life. Their chemistry was undeniable. They got married after ten months of dating.

But soon, Mariana realized that Julio didn't like to pray together, never shared his struggles, and rarely asked for her opinion. He, on the other hand, began to feel that she was too "clingy," too "emotional," and always expecting him to be someone he wasn't.

After a year of growing distance, they found themselves talking more to their phones than to each other. Their love had once felt magical. Now it just felt... heavy.

They loved each other. But their love was not enough. Because it lacked something essential: *God's foundation, emotional maturity, and spiritual compatibility.*

A Love Worth Waiting: Hapily Ever After

5 Silent Killers of Marriage

1. **Emotional Immaturity.** Marriage doesn't fix immaturity — it exposes it.

A person who shuts down during conflict won't become a great communicator after the wedding. Someone who refuses to take responsibility while dating won't suddenly grow accountability in marriage.

"It is often the case that blindly passionate youth marry in haste, only to repent in leisure." — Ellen G. White, Messages to Young People, p. 452

Marriage requires adult-level responsibility: emotional regulation, sacrifice, humility, and grace. If one or both enter the covenant emotionally underdeveloped, the relationship suffocates under emotional chaos.

2. **Spiritual Neglect.** A marriage without prayer is a marriage vulnerable to pressure.

"Can two walk together, except they be agreed?" - Amos 3:3

Spiritual disunity is one of the most underestimated but devastating causes of conflict. When one spouse wants to grow closer to God and the other resists, it creates a slow emotional erosion that often ends in silence or resentment.

Spiritual neglect also makes couples more vulnerable to temptation, compromise, and emotional isolation.

3. **The Idol of Passion.** Too many confuse infatuation with love. They believe intensity equals intimacy. But real love is not measured by butterflies — it's measured by **choice**.

"True love is a high and holy principle, altogether different in character from that love which is awakened by impulse and which suddenly dies when severely tested." — (*The Adventist Home*, p. 50)

When the rush of passion fades, some couples find they've built nothing underneath. No friendship. No trust. No shared mission. Only memories of romantic highs — and the painful contrast of emotional lows.

4. **Poor Conflict Resolution.** Many marriages die not from the presence of conflict — but from the inability to resolve it.

Studies from Dr. John Gottman reveal that couples who stay married aren't those who never fight — but those who **learn how to fight fair**. They listen. Apologize. Forgive. Grow. Marriages fall apart when both partners either explode... or withdraw.

A Love Worth Waiting: Hapily Ever After

"He that is slow to anger is better than the mighty; and he that ruleth his spirit than he that taketh a city." – (*Proverbs* 16:32)

5. **Ignoring Red Flags.** Most broken marriages were once broken courtships — but no one wanted to say it out loud.

So many people knew it wouldn't work. The friends saw it. The parents saw it. Even the person walking down the aisle had a whisper in their soul that said: *"This isn't peace."*

But they pushed forward anyway — driven by time invested, fear of loneliness, or pride.

"Better, far better, break the engagement before marriage than separate afterward, as many do." — (*The Adventist Home*, p. 48)

Did You Know?

Research from the National Marriage Project shows that couples who cohabitate before marriage are **33% more likely to divorce** than those who wait until after marriage to live together. Why? Because commitment formed out of convenience often lacks the foundation of intentional, prayerful decision-making. — Source: National Marriage Project, University of Virginia

God's Blueprint for Love That Lasts

This perspective invites you to view marriage not as a mere means of survival but as a dynamic, transforming covenant that mirrors Christ's love for His Church—marked by patience, sacrifice, and faithfulness.

Embracing a Love Intended to Flourish

God doesn't design marriage simply for two people to coexist day by day. Instead, His blueprint envisions a union that radiates His redeeming character. In His plan, marriage is not about just managing life's challenges but about *thriving* together. When a marriage reflects Christ's love for the Church, it becomes a vibrant testimony of His grace, drawing others to the beauty of sacrificial and enduring love.

Ephesians 5:25 clearly declares: "Husbands, love your wives, even as Christ also loved the church, and gave himself for it."

This verse encapsulates the radical, self-giving love that should define a covenant marriage. It calls the husband to mirror the unconditional love of Christ—a love that embraces sacrifice, forgiveness, and steadfast commitment. In turn, the marriage as a whole becomes an active reflection of Christ's relationship with His Church.

A Love Worth Waiting: Hapily Ever After

Transformation Through Trials

Marriage is a journey that tests and refines every aspect of your character. As you step into this covenant, you will inevitably face challenges that stretch your patience and expose your selfish tendencies. These trials are not indicators of failure but opportunities for growth.

- **Character Refinement:** Partnership in marriage will reveal areas where you need to grow — your temper, impatience, or reluctance to forgive. Yet, these moments are also chances to learn humility, practice grace, and put love into action. Instead of succumbing to frustration, lean on prayer and Scripture as your guide to transform shortcomings into strengths.

- **Growth of Patience:** The daily choice to love sacrificially calls for patience that only deep, selfless love can nurture. As you face both big challenges and little irritations, remember that each opportunity to persevere is further evidence of God molding you into the likeness of Christ.

- **Healing and Renewal:** When Christ is the center of your marriage, His healing touch can mend deep wounds. Whether the hurt comes from past disappointments or ongoing struggles within the relationship, His grace offers restoration that deepens joy and fortifies love. In this way, every trial becomes a stepping stone to a more profound, mature intimacy.

A Covenant That Reflects Christ's Love

God's blueprint for love demands that marriage go beyond superficial romance. It envisions a relationship where every facet of life is infused with spiritual purpose:

- **Patient and Sacrificial Love:** Your marriage is called to be a living sermon—one that proclaims forgiveness, service, and unwavering commitment. As you practice this love, you bear witness to the patient endurance of Christ, who willingly laid down His life for the Church.

- **A Heart of Faithfulness:** Even when challenges seem insurmountable, keeping Christ at the center transforms every hardship into an opportunity for faith. This steadfastness not only deepens your bond but also nurtures a love that heals and sustains over time.

- **Growth in Joy and Depth:** With Christ as your cornerstone, the inevitable stretches of marriage become a landscape where joy blossoms—even amidst trials. By continually aligning your hearts with God's love, you invite more depth, intimacy, and the healing of any past wounds.

A Love Worth Waiting: Hapily Ever After

In this way, marriage serves as a canvas upon which God paints His masterful design—a design that is at once delicate, powerful, and eternally redemptive.

God's Blueprint for Love That Lasts challenges you to see marriage as a sacred, transformative journey rather than a mere survival mechanism. Through trials that refine your character, moments that teach patience, and a foundation built on the sacrificial love of Christ, your marriage can flourish into a radiant reflection of His Church. Embrace the challenges as opportunities to deepen your love, heal your wounds, and truly mirror the eternal love that God has for all His children.

May this reflection inspire you to build a marriage not merely to survive, but to shine as a true image of Christ's enduring, patient, and transformative love.

Prayer

Lord, teach me what real love looks like. Not the world's version — but Yours. Help me grow into the kind of person who can love like You do: sacrificially, wisely, patiently. Heal me where I am immature. Anchor me where I am unstable. And prepare me — or strengthen me — for a marriage built on the Rock. Amen.

A Love Worth Waiting: Hapily Ever After

Reflection Questions

1. What habits or wounds would sabotage a marriage if not addressed now?

2. How spiritually united am I (or would I be) with the person I hope to marry?

3. Have I ever mistaken passion for lasting love?

4. Do I listen, apologize, and forgive — or shut down when things get hard?

Journal Prompt

Think about the version of yourself you'd want your future spouse to meet. What character traits would make you a better husband or wife? What kind of love would you give? What kind of healing would you need?

Chapter 4
The Cracks Before the Covenant: Unhealed Wounds in Sacred Unions

"If the foundations be destroyed, what can the righteous do?" – Psalm 11:3, KJV

Before the Altar, There Was Already Pain

Before they said "I do," there were things they didn't.

He didn't talk about his father's abandonment. She didn't share her fear of being unloved. They laughed, loved, planned their wedding... but never truly revealed their hearts. So when the storms came, their foundation cracked – not because of what happened in marriage, but because of what was left unhealed before it.

"Thousands are mated but not matched. The books of heaven are burdened with the wretched results of hasty marriages." — Ellen G. White, *Messages to Young People*, p. 452

In this chapter, we uncover what few want to admit: many marriages don't fail because of what couples do to each other — but because of what they never healed *in themselves.*

Story: The Fight Beneath the Surface

Ricardo and Eliana loved each other deeply. But every disagreement spiraled into yelling. Ricardo would shut down and isolate. Eliana would accuse and cling. Over time, love turned into tension.

In counseling, it became clear: Ricardo had grown up in a home where conflict meant danger. His father's temper terrified him. So now, when conflict arose, he escaped — emotionally and physically.

Eliana, however, had been emotionally neglected as a child. Her father was kind but distant. Her greatest fear? Being ignored. So when Ricardo withdrew, she panicked and escalated.

They weren't reacting to each other — they were reacting to their *wounds.*

Hidden Cracks That Break a Covenant

Below is an in-depth exploration focusing on unhealed trauma, insecure attachment, distorted views of marriage, and bitterness and unforgiveness. These truths reveal that deep inner wounds and misaligned perceptions can profoundly impact our ability to experience and extend God's love in our relationships. Yet recognizing these challenges offers the first step

A Love Worth Waiting: Hapily Ever After

toward healing and transformation before or within a surrendered union.

1. Unhealed Trauma

Trauma—whether stemming from abuse, neglect, betrayal, or abandonment—profoundly alters the way we love. It can leave us guarded, anxious, reactive, or even overly dependent. As reflected in a caution from *The Adventist Home* (p. 70): "All who enter the marriage relation should be fully prepared to assume its responsibilities. But Satan is busily engaged in hurrying youth into marriage before they have experience and maturity."

Marriage, in itself, does not have the miraculous power to heal these wounds; rather, it can magnify them if the trauma remains unaddressed. True healing must come through an intimate, redemptive relationship with God. Without that spiritual healing—whether through pastoral care, counseling, or personal devotion—the unresolved scars of trauma can color every aspect of your relationship. In this light, it becomes essential to confront and process past hurt with God's transformative grace before inviting that brokenness into a covenant of intimacy.

2. Insecure Attachment

Attachment theory reminds us that the bonds we form in childhood often echo into our adult relationships. Psychologists describe several attachment styles:

- **Anxious attachment:** characterized by a constant fear of abandonment.

- **Avoidant attachment:** marked by a fear of becoming too close.

- **Disorganized attachment:** a mixture of both, often resulting from traumatic early experiences.

- **Secure attachment:** where individuals learn to love and trust while maintaining healthy boundaries.

When one or both partners do not feel safe in love, they may unconsciously sabotage the relationship. Insecure attachment creates an environment where mistrust and anxiety persist. Scripture offers both comfort and correction in 1 John 4:18: "There is no fear in love; but perfect love casteth out fear: because fear hath torment."

A secure foundation—one rooted in God's perfect love—requires that both partners work toward healing old wounds and learning to trust again. This work might involve personal healing, counseling, or jointly pursuing spiritual and relational growth so that fear no longer dictates the terms of love.

A Love Worth Waiting: Hapily Ever After

3. Distorted Views of Marriage

Many of us have grown up witnessing broken models of marriage. These distorted views can imprint patterns of control, silence, and power struggles—even when we consciously reject them. *The Adventist Home* (p. 21) proclaims: "The home should be to the children the most attractive place in the world, and the mother's presence should be its greatest charm."

Without intentional rewiring of our mindset, we often unconsciously replicate the negative dynamics we observed in our formative years. Rather than modeling the selfless, gracious love exemplified by Christ, we may fall into familiar, destructive patterns. Reclaiming a healthy view of marriage requires a deliberate reorientation—to see marriage as a covenant relationship grounded in mutual respect, sacrifice, and the renewing power of God's grace. As you intentionally study Scripture, seek counsel, and immerse yourself in Christ-centered examples, your perception of what marriage should be can shift from a broken model to one of divine possibility.

4. Bitterness and Unforgiveness

Unresolved anger—whether directed at an ex, a parent, or oneself—can leak into all aspects of life, poisoning relationships from the inside out. Bitterness is like a root; if left unremoved, it multiplies and spreads, affecting not only your emotional well-being but also

A Love Worth Waiting: Hapily Ever After

the health of your marriage. Hebrews 12:15 warns us: "Looking diligently lest any man fail of the grace of God; lest any root of bitterness springing up trouble you, and thereby many be defiled."

When bitterness takes hold, it creates a cycle of unforgiveness that undermines trust and intimacy. This is why daily, intentional forgiveness is essential. Embracing God's forgiveness means choosing to release past hurts instead of allowing them to dictate your present. True freedom in love comes when you uproot bitterness and replace it with grace, understanding, and the healing that only Christ can bring.

The challenges of unhealed trauma, insecure attachment, distorted views of marriage, and bitterness and unforgiveness stand as profound obstacles to experiencing the fullness of God's love in our relationships. While these issues can magnify and disrupt a marriage, they also signal the urgent need for inner healing—a healing that must come from a surrendered and intimate relationship with God. Coming to terms with these truths and actively seeking transformation prepares you to build a resilient union, Christ-centered, and capable of enduring every storm with grace and compassion.

May this reflection empower you to confront these challenges with prayerful courage, to seek the fullness of God's healing, and to build relationships that reflect His transformative love.

A Love Worth Waiting: Hapily Ever After

Did You Know?

According to the **American Psychological Association**, couples with unresolved childhood trauma are **3 times more likely** to divorce, and significantly more likely to experience emotional distancing, addiction, or abusive cycles.

But couples who address emotional wounds — individually or together — are more likely to build resilient, lasting marriages. — APA, Trauma & Marriage Study, 2019

How to Repair the Cracks Before They Collapse the Home

1. **Do the inner work before the outer wedding.** Ask yourself: Have I truly faced my story? ¿Do I know how my past shaped my patterns?

2. **Seek godly counseling — not just romantic feelings.** Therapy, spiritual mentoring, and self-awareness are gifts from God. Use them.

3. **Invite Jesus into your memories.** Some wounds can't be fixed by logic. Only grace can reach them.

4. **Heal before you promise.** The strongest vows are made by whole people — or people on the journey of healing.

A Love Worth Waiting: Hapily Ever After

"None should be allowed to marry until they have laid the foundation of an intelligent Christian character" (*Messages to Young People*, p. 439).

Prayer

Lord, you see my story — every hidden wound, every unspoken tear. I no longer want to carry what You died to heal. Help me face the broken places, not in shame, but with courage. Build me up in You, so I may love like You. And if I am to marry, let it be as a whole soul, ready to love deeply and wisely. Amen.

Reflection Questions

1. What personal wounds might I carry into a future marriage?

2. Have I healed from past betrayal, abandonment, or abuse?

3. In what ways does my family of origin still shape my relationships today?

4. Who is walking with me on my healing journey?

📝 Journal Prompt

Write a letter to your past self — the version of you that was wounded, afraid, or confused. Speak words of truth, healing, and affirmation. Then write what kind of love you want to build now — and what must heal for it to happen.

Chapter 5
Building on Sand: Why Passion Without Principle Destroys Marriage

"Whosoever cometh to me, and heareth my sayings, and doeth them... is like a man which built an house... upon a rock... But he that heareth, and doeth not, is like a man that without a foundation built an house upon the earth; against which the stream did beat vehemently, and immediately it fell." – Luke 6:47–49

When Fire Isn't Enough

They couldn't keep their hands off each other. Their texts burned with longing. Their late-night talks stretched until dawn. "We just *click*," they said. Their passion was intoxicating.

But six months into marriage, that fire turned into arguments. Jealousy. Control. Silence.

The same passion that once brought them together now set everything on fire.

Why?

Because they built a relationship on chemistry without character, on romance without righteousness, on fire without foundation.

And when you build on emotional sand, the first storm will knock everything down.

Story: The Highs That Became Hurts

Angela and Mateo met at a music festival. She said she had never met someone who "just got her" the way Mateo did. They talked for hours, went deep fast, and declared their love within two weeks.

They moved in together before the year ended. But passion quickly turned into possession. Every time Angela made a new friend, Mateo grew angry. He needed constant reassurance. And when they fought, it was explosive.

They thought they were just "intense," "passionate," and "artistic." But what they really had been was an *unhealed trauma, lust-driven connection, and zero spiritual grounding.*

The house looked romantic. But it was built on sand.

5 Warning Signs You're Building on Sand

These warning signs call attention not only to superficial passion or romance, but to more in-depth issues that can weaken the very foundation of your relationship. When a relationship is built on shifting values, unchecked impulses, or by ignoring God's gentle warnings, it risks crumbling when challenges arise. May these insights guide you to pursue a love that is built on purpose, self-control, and spiritual intimacy.

1. Passion Over Purpose

Love without purpose is like a car with no destination—it may travel fast, ignited by emotions, but it soon loses direction. Too often, relationships are driven solely by the heat of passion, without a unifying goal or commitment to a higher calling. As noted in *The Adventist Home* (p. 50): "True love is a high and holy principle, altogether different in character from that love which is awakened by impulse, and which suddenly dies when severely tested."

God-designed love is not simply an eruption of hormones or poetic emotion; it is purposeful. It's meant to serve, to foster personal and mutual growth, and to reflect the sacrificial love of Christ. Before investing in a relationship, consider whether the passion you feel is aligned with a deeper purpose—to honor God and to serve one another in the way He intends.

2. Romance Without Self-Control

In today's culture, following one's heart is often celebrated above all else. However, Scripture provides a counterbalance. Proverbs 25:28 sharply warns: "He that hath no rule over his own spirit is like a city that is broken down, and without walls."

A relationship that lacks self-control is not built on true love, but on fleeting self-indulgence. Without established boundaries, romance can quickly devolve into impulsive behavior that violates your values. When passion constantly trumps your better judgment, you risk not only personal harm but also jeopardizing the integrity of your relationship. True romance respects the boundaries set by God and nurtures a love that is both honorable and safe.

3. Emotional Whiplash

A relationship marked by extreme swings—where one moment you are soaring on ecstasy and the next sinking into despair—is a sign that something deeper is amiss. Emotional highs and lows may feel passionate, but they can often be symptoms of trauma bonds rather than genuine intimacy. As trauma specialist Dr. Patrick Carnes describes, trauma bonds are:

"Intense cycles of reward and punishment that create obsessive attachment."

This kind of "love" is frequently fear wrapped in passion—a pattern driven more by unresolved wounds than by mutual care. If your relationship leaves you feeling emotionally unmoored, it is time to pause, seek healing, and establish a more stable foundation where consistent love replaces volatile highs and lows.

4. Physical Intimacy Replacing Spiritual Intimacy

While physical attraction is a natural and wonderful aspect of romance, it must not replace the deeper bedrock of spiritual intimacy. Sexual chemistry alone does not equate to emotional safety or spiritual compatibility. Ellen G. White, in *Messages to Young People* (p. 452), warns:

"Those who indulge the passions which should be held in check by reason and conscience are never safe. They are often jealous, sensitive, and unreasonable."

A solid relationship positions prayer before pleasure and God before gratification. Without cultivating a spiritual connection, physical intimacy can become an empty substitute for true closeness. Prioritizing spiritual unity through joint prayer, reflection on Scripture, and shared worship builds a resilient bond that protects against the distractions and dangers of mere physical desire.

5. Ignoring the Still, Small Voice

In the midst of overwhelming attraction, it is all too easy to silence the gentle, persistent warnings of God. Often, when we rush ahead in a relationship, we

A Love Worth Waiting: Hapily Ever After

persuade ourselves, "God will bless it anyway," ignoring the still, small voice of conviction. Yet Scripture reminds us that God does not bless what we hide from Him. When that quiet counsel is ignored, the relationship edges closer to instability.

Take time to listen—to both your heart and to God's whisper. Regular prayer and meditation on His Word help you discern whether your steps are in line with His will. Paying attention to that still small voice ensures that your relationship moves deliberately and with divine confirmation.

Building a relationship on shifting sands—where passion overshadows purpose, self-control is sidelined, emotions swing unrelentingly, physical pleasure replaces spiritual intimacy, and God's warnings are ignored—leaves you vulnerable to collapse when challenges arise. Instead, choose to build on the firm rock of purposeful, self-disciplined, and Spirit-led love. By aligning your relationship with God's design, you create a secure foundation that can withstand life's inevitable storms and truly reflect the love of Christ.

May these reflections help discern whether your relationship stands on the solid rock of God's truth or on the shifting sands of unchecked emotion and misplaced values. Choose wisely, and seek the guidance of the Holy Spirit as you build a love that lasts.

A Love Worth Waiting: Hapily Ever After

Did You Know?

According to a study from the *Journal of Sex Research*, couples who become sexually involved early in the relationship (within the first 2 months) are **more likely to experience conflict, insecurity, and eventual dissatisfaction** in their marriage.

Waiting doesn't just honor God — it also builds trust, clarity, and long-term commitment. — Source: Busby, Carroll, & Willoughby, 2010. *Journal of Sex Research*

How to Build on the Rock Instead

Below is an in-depth, personal reflection on "How to Build on the Rock Instead." Just as a solid foundation keeps a building secure through every storm, so too does a relationship built on God's principles stand firm in life's uncertainties. May this guide not merely inform you but inspire you to pursue a union rooted in divine wisdom and holistic growth.

1. **Let friendship grow before intimacy begins.** True compatibility is revealed in the quiet moments of shared life — not merely when the thrill of passion ignites. Begin your journey by cultivating deep friendship; learn each other's dreams, pain, and purpose. In genuine friendship, you find that your character and God's imprint on your life are on clear display. Consider a couple who chooses to meet regularly for coffee walks, discussing spiritual books and personal testimonies, rather than rushing into physical intimacy. In doing so, you

both model the gentle truth of Proverbs 17:17: "A friend loveth at all times, and a brother is born for adversity.

This practice doesn't delay joy but allows God's design to flourish step by step, establishing real compatibility that transcends mere surface attraction.

2. **Set Clear Boundaries — And Protect Them.** A relationship that honors God is one characterized by clear, lovingly enforced limits. When boundaries are set, both partners safeguard their hearts from temptation and the corrosive effects of shame. This is not about restriction, but about cultivating holiness that deepens intimacy. For example, consider a couple who intentionally establishes guidelines for physical expressions of love until they are ready for marriage; such prudence nurtures respect and honor.

As 1 Corinthians 6:18 advises, "Flee fornication. Every sin that a man doeth is without the body; but he that committeth fornication sinneth against his own body."

Ellen G. White teaches that sanctification is both the essence and the goal of intimate relationships. When you protect your boundaries, you ensure that what is built is uplifting rather than destructive—a foundation where shame finds no purchase.

3. **Invite Mentors into Your Relationship.** There is profound wisdom in opening your relationship to accountability and godly counsel. No love built on truth is afraid to involve mentors—be they spiritual leaders, trusted pastors, or wise parents—because transparency invites growth. Imagine a couple facing a crossroad in their decision-making who reach out to a seasoned church elder. Through shared guidance, they fortify their bond and learn to navigate challenges with grace.

   As Proverbs 15:22 states, "Without counsel purposes are disappointed: but in the multitude of counsellors, they are established."

   Ellen G. White reminds us that real love rejoices in accountability. Inviting mentors sends a clear message: your relationship is strong enough to welcome honest, constructive critique, for love is not afraid of accountability—it thrives on it.

4. **Slow Down and Listen to God's Peace.** Modern society often hurries toward the next big moment, yet in matters of the heart, haste can obscure God's voice. Take time to pause and tune your hearts to the divine peace He offers. Reflect on each decision as a couple, asking: "Does this choice bring us deeper into His will?" Consider a moment when one partner feels pulled in a new direction: instead

of racing into action, they retreat for prayer and quiet reflection, inviting the gentle affirmation of God's presence. Jesus tells us in Matthew 19:6, "What therefore God hath joined together, let not man put asunder."

And though the promise of unbreakable unity is clear, remember that not all projects of our hearts receive the seal of divine peace. When that peace is absent, it may be a sign that God is redirecting you away from an ill-timed union. By slowing down, you honor the truth that what He joins, no one can separate, yet He does not endorse everything we hastily start.

5. **Grow Your Spiritual Life More Than Your Romantic Life.** Romantic relationships can bring joy and companionship, but they are never meant to replace the relationship we are called to build with God. When we focus more on our spiritual growth, we align ourselves with His purpose and find fulfillment that no human connection can replicate. Instead of seeking validation in romance, seek to deepen your understanding of God's love and what it means to live in His presence daily. By centering Him in your life, you allow His wisdom and guidance to shape not only your spiritual walk, but also your approach to love and relationships.

Prioritizing spiritual growth gives you the clarity to see relationships in their proper perspective. It equips you with patience, discernment, and a heart centered

A Love Worth Waiting: Hapily Ever After

on God's will rather than fleeting emotions or personal desires. Use this time to invest in habits that strengthen your connection to Him—prayer, scripture study, acts of service, and worship. When your spiritual life flourishes, your relationships become an extension of God's love, built on a foundation of mutual respect, faith, and purpose.

Finally, remember that God uses seasons of singleness or waiting as opportunities for growth and preparation. Instead of focusing solely on what's missing romantically, embrace this time as a gift to build your identity and character in Christ. Whether you're single or in a relationship, prioritize becoming the person God has called you to be. By growing spiritually, you allow His love to fill your heart and overflow into every aspect of your life, including your romantic relationships.

6. **Finally, let your relationship be an expression of spiritual maturity rather than an escape into solely romantic ideals.** A couple that prioritizes God's work over the ephemeral excitement of romance becomes a powerful force in His kingdom. Invest in your individual and mutual spiritual growth—study Scripture together, serve in your church, and commit to prayer. As you do this, you echo Peter's call in 1 Peter 1:16 "Because it is written, Be ye holy; for I am holy."

A Love Worth Waiting: Hapily Ever After

A practical example can be seen in a couple that sets aside time each week for devotional studies and volunteering. Their joy is found in mutual sanctification rather than in fleeting gestures of affection.

As noted in *The Adventist Home* (p. 95), "The purest joy springs from the deepest sanctification."

This spiritual grounding enriches your individual lives and radiates in your shared relationship, making you a beacon of hope and example within your community.

Building on the rock means establishing a relationship that is more than just fleeting emotions—it is a commitment to letting God's truth and love serve as the bedrock for every decision and every exchange. When friendship precedes intimacy, boundaries are respected, mentors are welcomed, and you continually seek God's peace and spiritual growth over momentary romance, you are building on the sure foundation that will sustain you through all of life's challenges.

May this blueprint encourage you to pursue a love that is thoughtful, accountable, and divinely inspired—a love that stands strong, regardless of whatever storms may come.

Slow down and listen to God's peace. What He joins, no one can separate. But He doesn't join everything we start.

A Love Worth Waiting: Hapily Ever After

7. **Grow your spiritual life more than your romantic life.** A spiritually mature couple is a powerful force in the kingdom of God.

"The purest joy springs from the deepest sanctification." — The Adventist Home, p. 95

Prayer

Lord, I don't want a love that burns out. I want a love that's built on You — slow, steady, and sacred. Teach me to guard my heart, to pursue purity, and to desire purpose over passion. Help me build on the Rock — not sand. Amen.

Reflection Questions

1. Am I more drawn to chemistry than character?
2. Have I crossed emotional or physical boundaries I now regret?
3. What are the spiritual values I want to build my relationship on?
4. Have I mistaken intensity for intimacy?

A Love Worth Waiting: Hapily Ever After

Journal Prompt

Reflect on the strongest "crush" or romantic relationship you've ever had. What fueled it — passion or principle? If you could start again, what would you do differently? Now imagine your ideal Christ-centered relationship. What's its foundation?

Chapter 6
The Silent Erosion: How Little Things Undermine a Marriage Before It Starts

"Take us the foxes, the little foxes, that spoil the vines: for our vines have tender grapes." – Song of Solomon 2:15

It Wasn't a Storm, It Was a Slow Leak

It didn't begin with a betrayal. There was no great explosion, no public scandal. Just a slow drifting apart — like sand slipping between fingers. She felt like he wasn't listening. He felt like he was always wrong. They stopped praying together. Then talking. Then touching.

And one day, they realized: the love hadn't died… it had simply eroded.

Most relationships don't end in flames. They end in *fading*. And what fades first are the *small things* — the habits of care, attention, kindness, and presence. When neglected, these "little foxes" ruin the vineyard of love.

A Love Worth Waiting: Hapily Ever After

Story: A Marriage of Details

Ana and Daniel were admired by everyone. Church leaders. Youth mentors. Beautiful wedding. But by year three, something shifted. Daniel would come home and go straight to his phone. Ana would quietly clean, waiting for conversation that never came.

Their arguments weren't explosive — just repetitive. "You don't notice me anymore." "You always assume the worst." "You don't respect my time."

They went to counseling. Their counselor said something that pierced them both: "You're not fighting to destroy each other. You're slowly forgetting how to love each other."

The Little Foxes That Spoil Great Love

Below is an expanded, in-depth exploration of **5 Warning Signs That Erode Intimacy in a Christian Marriage**. Each of these signs points to subtle yet destructive habits that can weaken the spiritual and emotional foundations of your relationship. By recognizing these warning signs, you can address them and rebuild the connection that God intends for your marriage.

1. Neglecting Spiritual Habits

Many Christian couples do not fall apart because they miss a church service—they falter when they lose their daily connection with God together. As Ellen G. White wrote in *The Adventist Home* (p. 29):

"A house without prayer is like a home without light."

When couples stop praying together, they lose the spiritual glue that binds them. The Holy Spirit, who serves as our Counselor, Comforter, and Mediator, is essential to maintaining unity. Without a consistent worship and prayer life, everyday differences and conflicts can quickly grow into deep divisions. Think of your daily habits as the essential nutrients for your marital soil; without them, even small issues can sprout into serious problems. Consistently engaging in Scripture study, prayer, and spiritual reflection together is not simply a routine—it's the lifeline that sustains and renews your union.

2. Micro-Disrespect

Disrespect in a marriage isn't always signaled by overt insults or loud arguments. Often, it slips in the form of micro-actions—interrupting, eye-rolling, dismissing your partner's feelings, "correcting" them publicly, or engaging in sarcastic teasing. Proverbs 15:1 reminds us:

"A soft answer turneth away wrath: but grievous words stir up anger."

These seemingly small slights may appear trivial at the moment, yet they steadily corrode intimacy and trust.

Respect, in a marriage, is like the rich soil in which trust and love are planted; without it, even the smallest root of contempt can fester. Each time you choose a gentle word over a snarky remark — or offer your partner your undivided attention rather than an interruptive comment — you are investing in the health of your relationship.

3. Inconsistent Communication

Communication is the lifeblood of any thriving relationship. A lapse in daily check-ins, thoughtful conversations, or even casual sharing of your day can be a subtle indicator that disconnection is setting in. Just as a garden is not killed by a fierce storm but by neglect and abandonment, a marriage suffers not only from harsh words but also from a lack of communication. When couples stop affirming one another, sharing their thoughts, or actively listening, they begin to drift apart. Intentional communication — being present and truly hearing one another — serves as the ongoing maintenance that keeps the garden of your relationship alive.

4. Busy Lives, Empty Love Tanks

In our modern, fast-paced world, work, church activities, and the demands of family and deadlines often crowd out genuine relational time. Over time, partners can find themselves operating like roommates rather than as soulmates. Dr. Gary Chapman, author of *The 5 Love Languages*, points out that couples who do not intentionally speak each other's emotional language will eventually feel unloved—even when both parties mean well. He stated, "Loveless marriages are not always the result of cruelty, but of carelessness."

When daily life becomes a series of tasks and responsibilities, and when intimate quality time is sacrificed, the "love tank" of each partner can run dry. It's essential to set intentional times to connect—whether through a shared meal, a quiet prayer session, or simply an uninterrupted conversation—to ensure that love is actively refueled.

5. Unspoken Expectations

Assumptions can be deadly in a relationship. When one partner believes, "She should know I'm tired," or "He should know I want flowers," unspoken expectations create walls of silent resentment. Love is not a mind-reading service—it thrives on clear, honest communication. When you expect your spouse to intuitively know your needs without them being spelled out, you risk building up unaddressed disappointment that slowly undermines intimacy. By communicating your needs openly and routinely checking in on what each other requires emotionally, you prevent these silent resentments from taking root.

A Love Worth Waiting: Hapily Ever After

Neglecting spiritual habits, allowing micro-disrespect, engaging in inconsistent communication, letting busy lives lead to empty love tanks, and harboring unspoken expectations are all warning signs that you may be building your marriage on unstable ground. Each of these issues can chip away at the foundation established by God if not carefully tended to. By intentionally prioritizing daily prayer, showing respect in every small act, engaging in meaningful dialogue, deliberately nurturing emotional connection, and voicing your needs, you build a resilient relationship that honors God's design for marriage.

May these reflections encourage you to examine and nurture every layer of your marriage, ensuring that what you build is as enduring and secure as solid rock.

Did You Know?

Gottman Institute research shows that couples who express appreciation at least **once per day** are significantly less likely to separate — even during high-stress seasons like raising children or financial strain.

And couples who pray together at least **3 times per week** report a **30% higher satisfaction rate** in both emotional and physical intimacy.

A Love Worth Waiting: Hapily Ever After

Restoring the Foundation — One Brick at a Time

Each daily practice is a brick that fortifies the structure of your relationship. When you take the time to intentionally rebuild and nurture your union, you honor each other and invite God's transformative grace into every corner of your life.

1. Daily Check-Ins: Ask, "How's Your Heart Today?"

The simple act of a daily check-in can lay a strong foundation for mutual understanding. It is an invitation to share—not just the details of the day, but the deep emotions, struggles, and victories that shape your inner life. Like the rhythmic beating of a heart, these brief moments of communication allow both partners to remain connected, even amid life's busyness.

As Psalm 139:23-24 earnestly pleads, "Search me, O God, and know my heart: try me, and know my thoughts." Imagine ending a hectic day by gently asking your partner about their heart; this small query offers an opportunity for vulnerability and intimacy, affirming that you value not just their actions, but their very soul. In the words of Ellen G. White, *"To know one another in heart and spirit is a precious blessing. It is in the quiet moments of reflection and honest sharing that true reconciliation begins."*

2. One Act of Appreciation Per Day: A Thank-You, A Hug, A Compliment

Tiny gestures of appreciation are like mortar binding the bricks of your foundation. Whether it's a sincere thank-you, an unexpected hug, or a heartfelt compliment, these acts nourish the soul and remind your partner that their worth is seen and cherished. As Romans 12:10 advises,

"Be kindly affectioned one to another with brotherly love; in honour preferring one another." Consider a day when a heartfelt compliment lifts your partner's spirit during a challenge—they feel affirmed, valued, and inspired to continue doing good. These daily acts of kindness build a reservoir of goodwill that can sustain your relationship through trials. Ellen G. White also emphasized the power of simple acts, noting that genuine kindness is "the very essence of Christian love which, when manifested, creates an environment where grace and joy flourish."

3. Scheduled Spiritual Time: Pray Together, Even for 2–3 Minutes

Devoting even a few minutes every day to praying, reading Scripture, and inviting God into your relationship is like pouring water onto the parched ground of your soul—making it receptive to growth and renewal. The discipline of daily spiritual time keeps your focus aligned with God's will and transforms your relationship into a sacred space. As 1 Thessalonians 5:17 urges us to,

"Pray without ceasing." Even if the moments shared are brief—a prayer before sleep or reading a single verse in the morning—this intentional spiritual practice sets a rhythm that permeates your entire day. For instance, scheduling a quiet moment after dinner to reflect together can turn an ordinary evening into a powerful testament of unity and faith. Ellen G. White once wrote, *"When couples unite in prayer, they form a bond which no worldly challenge can sever."*

4. Apologize Quickly, Forgive Fully: Don't Let Little Injuries Fester

In every relationship, missteps and misunderstandings are inevitable. However, the true strength of your foundation is measured by how swiftly you can offer an apology and extend forgiveness. Choosing to address grievances immediately prevents hurt from becoming bitter and allows healing to take root. Ephesians 4:32 reminds us,

"And be ye kind one to another, tenderhearted, forgiving one another, even as God for Christ's sake hath forgiven you." Consider a scenario where a careless word causes temporary pain—by apologizing quickly and forgiving fully, you clear away the accumulated dust on your relationship's brickwork. In doing so, you ensure that each issue is resolved before it has the chance to compromise the integrity of your union. Ellen G. White noted that *"The willingness to forgive is the mark of true Christian character, bridging gaps and paving the way for fresh starts."*

5. Speak Each Other's Love Language: Embrace What Feels Unnatural for the Sake of Growth

Every individual is uniquely wired to receive love in a distinct way. Whether it is through words of affirmation, acts of service, quality time, physical touch, or even gifts, learning to speak your partner's love language is essential—even if it feels unfamiliar at first. As you begin to adapt your expressions of love to match their inner needs, you affirm their identity and cultivate deeper intimacy. Although the Bible does not explicitly list love languages, the spirit of mutual care and understanding is clear in 1 Corinthians 13, which extols the virtues of love that "bears all things, believes all things, hopes all things, endures all things." Imagine a partner who thrives on verbal commendation; when you deliberately articulate your admiration and gratitude, you help them feel seen and appreciated in a way that resonates powerfully. This intentional practice may require stepping outside your comfort zone, but its rewards are profound. Ellen G. White pointed out that *"The love that is communicated with care and understanding transforms hearts and builds a dwelling place where hope can be safely harbored."*

Restoring your relationship is much like rebuilding a structure—each brick, every word, and all acts of kindness play a crucial role in creating a durable,

A Love Worth Waiting: Hapily Ever After

lasting foundation. Daily check-ins, acts of appreciation, shared moments of prayer, quick apologies coupled with heartfelt forgiveness, and speaking each other's love language are the deliberate steps that restore and renew your bond. This process is not solely about mending what is broken but about evolving into a partnership that mirrors God's steadfast love and grace.

May these intentional practices serve as your guide, brick by brick, in restoring your relationship to a place of beauty, resilience, and divine purpose.

May this guide inspire you to rebuild your relationship with patience, intentionality, and grace—knowing that every sincere effort is a brick in the foundation for a love that endures.

"Let love be without dissimulation. Abhor that which is evil; cleave to that which is good. Be kindly affectioned one to another with brotherly love; in honour preferring one another." - Romans 12:9-10

Prayer

Lord, forgive me for the little things I've neglected — the unspoken thank-you, the unsent texts, the unsprayed prayers. Heal what I've allowed to fade. Teach me how to love intentionally. Let my marriage (or future one) be a sanctuary of grace, built one kind word at a time. Amen.

A Love Worth Waiting: Hapily Ever After

Reflection Questions

1. What "little foxes" have been sneaking into my current (or future) relationship?

2. How am I feeding or starving emotional intimacy?

3. Do I ask for what I need — or silently expect it?

4. Do I still pursue connection — or assume they'll always be there?

Journal Prompt

List three small daily habits you could begin today that would bless your current or future spouse. Then write a short "thank you" letter to someone who's loved you in the little things.

Chapter 7
When Red Flags Wear White Dresses: Discernment Before You Say 'I Do'

"Beloved, believe not every spirit, but try the spirits whether they are of God..." – 1 John 4:1, KJV

When Charm Becomes a Trap

He held her hand, quoted Scripture, led youth worship, and even fasted with her.

But once married, the charm vanished. The prayers stopped. Control replaced kindness. Her voice was silenced, her boundaries crushed. She whispered through tears one night, *"He wasn't who I thought he was."*

But he was. She just didn't want to see it.

This is the dangerous truth: **red flags often wear white dresses and black suits**. They smile. They serve. They speak Christianese. But beneath it all lies manipulation, insecurity, or unrepented sin — waiting to reveal itself in marriage.

Discernment isn't suspicion. It's **spiritual vision** — a gift God gives to those willing to see, even when it hurts.

A Love Worth Waiting: Hapily Ever After

Story: It Was There All Along

Sofia was smitten by Andrés from the start. He was a deacon, knew his Bible, and brought her flowers every Sabbath. But she felt uneasy every time he snapped at waiters, belittled her friends, or got defensive when she questioned something.

Her mentor warned her gently: "Sweetheart, he's a leader, but not a listener. Don't ignore that."

But Sofia didn't want to lose the dream. She married him anyway.

Two years in, she felt like a prisoner — living with a man who cared more about appearances than repentance.

"I wasn't deceived," she told her therapist one day. "I just closed my eyes."

7 Red Flags the Holy Spirit Wants You to See

1. A Spiritual Image Without Fruit

"Wherefore by their fruits ye shall know them." - Matthew 7:20

Going to church doesn't equal knowing Christ. Quoting Scripture isn't the same as living it. Does this person exhibit *love, joy, peace, patience, kindness, faithfulness, self-control* (Galatians 5:22–23)?

If not — they may be spiritually performing, not spiritually growing.

2. Jealousy and Control Disguised as Protection

"He just cares about me." "She just doesn't trust people."

But if you have to **ask permission** to be yourself, that's not love — that's control.

"Where the Spirit of the Lord is, there is liberty." - 2 Corinthians 3:17

True love brings peace, not fear. Space, not surveillance.

3. Isolation from Godly Relationships

If your partner tries to cut you off from your mentors, church family, or spiritual counsel — run.

Isolation is the breeding ground for manipulation. Healthy relationships encourage **connection**, not control.

4. Inability to Apologize or Take Responsibility

If every conversation turns into blame, deflection, or gaslighting — that's not immaturity, that's a **dangerous character pattern.**

"He that covereth his sins shall not prosper: but whoso confesseth and forsaketh them shall have mercy." - Proverbs 28:13

A partner who cannot apologize will eventually become a partner who cannot be trusted.

5. Pressure Toward Physical Intimacy

No matter how spiritual someone sounds, if they push your boundaries — they are *not* walking in the Spirit.

"For this is the will of God, even your sanctification, that ye should abstain from fornication." - 1 Thessalonians 4:3

A person walking with God will protect your purity — not tempt it.

6. Chronic Anger or Mood Swings

Everyone gets upset. But if their reaction is regularly **explosive, passive-aggressive,** or **emotionally abusive**, do not minimize it.

A Love Worth Waiting: Hapily Ever After

Marriage will **amplify** their habits — not soften them.

7. Disregard for Godly Counsel

"In the multitude of counsellors there is safety." - Proverbs 11:14

If your pastors, parents, or spiritual mentors raise concerns, don't rush past their words. Wise people **welcome counsel**. Fools are offended by it.

Did You Know?

A study in *Personality and Social Psychology Bulletin* revealed that people in emotionally manipulative or controlling relationships often report **ignoring early warning signs** due to loneliness, insecurity, or "optimism bias." — Source: Joel, S., & MacDonald, G. (2013)

God gave you a conscience, the Holy Spirit, and a community of faith for a reason. Use them.

What Discernment Looks Like

1. **It listens more than it talks.** It asks: What is this person like when they're not performing?

2. **It watches character over charisma.** Charm may open the door. But only character can keep it open.

A Love Worth Waiting: Hapily Ever After

3. **It invites wise people into the process.** If your love can't handle accountability, it's not love. It's delusion.

4. **It prays for clarity over comfort.** God will never confuse you into marriage. His peace passes understanding — not sense.

"The meek will he guide in judgment: and the meek will he teach his way." - Psalm 25:9

Prayer

Lord, open my eyes. Even if it hurts, even if it costs me a dream — I'd rather walk alone than bind myself to someone You never called me to. Give me discernment, courage, and a listening spirit. Let me not be blinded by charm, but guided by Your truth. Amen.

Reflection Questions

1. Have I seen red flags in someone but explained them away?

2. Am I rushing into love because of fear or pressure?

3. Do I invite wise voices to speak into my relationship?

4. What does the Holy Spirit truly say about this person?

A Love Worth Waiting: Hapily Ever After

≋ Journal Prompt

Write a list of non-negotiable values your future (or current) partner must hold. Then write a prayer asking God to give you **spiritual discernment and the courage to walk away** from what may look good, but is not good for you.

A Love Worth Waiting: Hapily Ever After

Chapter 8
Soul Ties and Sacred Bonds: Emotional Connections that Heal or Harm

"Know ye not that he which is joined to an harlot is one body? for two, saith he, shall be one flesh. But he that is joined unto the Lord is one spirit." – 1 Corinthians 6:16-17

Tied to the Wrong Person

Andrea hadn't seen him in years. She was married now, loved by a godly man, yet something haunted her.

Whenever she saw a man who looked like Marcos — her first love — her heart would tighten. Not because she wanted him back… but because she had never fully let him go.

Their connection had been deep — emotionally, physically, spiritually. And although the relationship ended, something invisible remained.

A soul tie.

We live in a culture that treats emotional intimacy like recreation and physical intimacy like a handshake. But God designed us to **bond**, not just touch. To **connect**, not just flirt. And when those bonds are formed outside

His will, they leave behind invisible cords — some holy, some harmful.

What Is a Soul Tie?

A soul tie is an emotional, spiritual, or physical bond between two people — often formed through deep emotional experiences, physical intimacy, or prolonged attachment.

There are **godly soul ties** — like those rooted in marriage, friendship, and family.

"The soul of Jonathan was knit with the soul of David, and Jonathan loved him as his own soul." - 1 Samuel 18:1

But there are also **ungodly soul ties** — formed through sexual sin, trauma, emotional dependency, or manipulative relationships.

Signs of an Unhealthy Soul Tie

Recognizing these signs is the first step toward healing and releasing the chains that may be keeping you from embracing God's freedom. May this guide encourage you to examine your emotional and spiritual life with honesty and invite the transforming power of Christ into every corner of your heart.

A Love Worth Waiting: Hapily Ever After

1. You Constantly Think About the Person — Even When You Don't Want To

When thoughts of a past relationship or person seemingly overrun your mind, even against your will, it is as if an uninvited guest occupies your inner sanctuary. God calls us to be the guardians of our hearts. As Proverbs 4:23 wisely warns,

"Keep thy heart with all diligence; for out of it are the issues of life." Consider someone who, despite efforts to move forward, finds their mind repeatedly drawn to memories of an old flame. This constant, intrusive remembrance is a red flag—a soul tie that has grown unhealthy, binding you with an invisible thread that hinders emotional freedom. Like unwanted weeds in a garden, these thoughts can choke the growth of new, God-honoring love. Reflect on the ways you can surrender these recurring thoughts to God in prayer, asking Him to renew your mind and fill you with His peace.

2. You Compare Everyone to Them — Emotionally or Sexually

In an emotionally healthy life, every new person you meet has the unique potential to bring fresh joy and perspective. However, when comparisons become a compulsive part of your life, it signals that an unhealthy soul tie is warping your view of relationships. The habit of measuring others against the memory of someone from the past can create an unlawful idol—a shadow that takes precedence over the beauty of God's best for you. In James 4:4 it is written,

"Ye adulterers and adulteresses, know ye not that the friendship of the world is enmity with God? Whosoever therefore wilt be a friend of the world is the enemy of God." Imagine a soul so tethered to one memory that every new encounter is burdened with comparison. This comparison diminishes the new relationship and distracts you from the unique plan God has for your emotional and spiritual journey. By acknowledging this pattern, you invite God's healing to replace comparison with genuine appreciation for the individuality He designs in each person.

3. You Feel Emotionally Controlled or Manipulated by Their Memory

There comes a point when a memory isn't just a recollection—it begins to hold sway over your emotions and decisions. Feeling controlled or manipulated by a past person's memory indicates that the tie has taken root in a place where God desires freedom. Colossians 3:2 (KJV) advises,

"Set your affection on things above, not on things on the earth." When a former love dictates your mood, actions, or self-worth, you are entangled in a bond that was never meant to imprison but to be healed. Imagine waking each day with a sense of obligation to revisit old hurts or ideals about what used to be; the memory itself sets limits on your ability to thrive. Recognize that while the past has its stories, Christ offers a path to emotional liberation. His redeeming love brings restoration so that you no longer allow outdated chains to dictate your present and future.

4. You're Still Angry, Bitter, or Obsessed — Long After the Relationship Ended

Ongoing anger, bitterness, or obsession can be a heavy burden, indicating that a soul tie has left behind wounds that remain unhealed. Ephesians 4:31-32 teaches us,

"Let all bitterness, and wrath, and anger, and clamour, and evil speaking, be put away from you, with all malice: And be ye kind one to another, tenderhearted, forgiving one another, even as God for Christ's sake hath forgiven you." Holding on to resentment or obsession overlooks Christ's command to forgive and move forward. Imagine someone who, long after a relationship has ended, finds their every thought and emotion centered on past hurt. That constant rehashing of pain not only damages the soul, but it also obstructs the joy and restoration that a new beginning in Christ can provide. Embracing God's forgiveness—and offering it to yourself—can set you free from the chains of bitter memories and open the door to healing.

5. You Feel Paralyzed at the Thought of Them Moving On — Even When You Have

A deep, unhealthy soul tie can induce a paralyzing fear of change. Even if you have started new paths in life, the thought of that person moving on can trigger anxiety, sadness, or resistance. Ezekiel 36:26 proclaims,

"A new heart also will I give you, and a new spirit will I put within you: and I will take away the stony heart out of your flesh, and I will give you a heart of flesh." Imagine feeling as if you are stuck in the past, unable to fully embrace the present or future because the mere idea of your ex-partner finding happiness elsewhere leaves you feeling insecure or incomplete. This immobilizing fear is a signal that the unhealthy tie still wields its influence. It is time to ask God for a new heart, one that is receptive to His healing and capable of experiencing fresh joy and freedom. By seeking His guidance and surrendering this fear, you allow God's transformative grace to break the chains of the past.

A Chain Broken by Christ

The words from *The Desire of Ages* encapsulates the hope we have: "Sin has bound human beings to Satan. But Christ came to break every chain." This profound truth reminds us that no matter how deeply an unhealthy soul tie has taken root, the redemptive power of Christ can liberate you from its grip. Embrace His promise, allow His love to renew your mind, and trust that every chain — no matter how sturdy — can be broken through His mercy.

Recognizing signs of an unhealthy soul tie is a courageous act of self-awareness. Whether it's incessant thoughts, constant comparisons, emotional manipulation, lingering bitterness, or paralyzing fear, these sorrows signal a call to spiritual and emotional restoration. In every case, turn to God in prayer, seek His wisdom through Scripture, and welcome the counsel of trusted mentors. Healing is not instantaneous, yet every step toward releasing these chains brings you one brick closer to a foundation built on freedom and divine love.

May this reflection empower you to recognize and break the unhealthy bonds of the past, replacing them with the liberating, healing embrace of Christ's love. As you embark on this journey of restoration, remember that every step you take toward emotional and spiritual freedom is a testament to God's unending grace and transformative power.

Did You Know?

Neuroscience shows that **oxytocin**, the bonding hormone released during deep emotional sharing and physical intimacy (especially sex), **literally creates neural pathways** in the brain — designed to make us feel connected and trusting.

This is beautiful in marriage — but destructive in casual or toxic relationships. The brain can't distinguish "this is not forever" — it bonds anyway. — Source: Dr. Daniel Amen, Change Your Brain, Change Your Life

How Soul Ties Form (Even Without Sex)

Soul ties are not always physical; they can be deeply emotional, spiritual, or psychological bonds that develop when intimacy lacks healthy boundaries. Recognizing these patterns is essential for guarding your heart and seeking God's guidance in your relationships.

1. Frequent Late-Night Deep Talks

Late-night conversations often create a sense of vulnerability and closeness that can lead to an emotional bond. While sharing your heart is not inherently wrong, doing so without discernment can blur boundaries and foster dependency. Proverbs 4:23 reminds us,

"Keep thy heart with all diligence; for out of it are the issues of life." Imagine a scenario where two friends frequently confide in each other late at night, sharing their deepest fears and dreams. Over time, this emotional intimacy can create a bond that feels almost unbreakable, even if it's not rooted in God's will. To prevent this, it's important to set boundaries and ensure that your deepest emotional sharing is reserved for relationships that honor God's design.

A Love Worth Waiting: Hapily Ever After

2. Emotional Trauma Shared in Isolation

When two people share emotional trauma in isolation, it can create a bond that feels like a lifeline, but may actually be unhealthy. This kind of connection often stems from a mutual need for comfort, but it can lead to co-dependency rather than healing. Ecclesiastes 4:9-10 teaches,

"Two are better than one; because they have a good reward for their labour. For if they fall, the one will lift up his fellow: but woe to him that is alone when he falleth; for he hath not another to help him up." While it's good to support one another, true healing comes from God and from seeking wise counsel. For example, two individuals who have experienced similar losses might lean on each other excessively, creating a bond that feels irreplaceable but ultimately hinders their individual growth. Seeking God's comfort and involving trusted mentors can help redirect this bond toward healthy restoration.

3. Repetitive Flirting or Co-Dependency

Flirting may seem harmless, but when it becomes repetitive, it can create an emotional tie that is difficult to break. Similarly, co-dependency—where one person relies excessively on the other for emotional support—can lead to an unhealthy attachment. 1 Corinthians 15:33 warns,

"Be not deceived: evil communications corrupt good manners." Consider a relationship where one person constantly seeks validation through flirtation, creating a cycle of emotional dependency. This dynamic distorts the relationship and distracts both individuals from pursuing God's purpose for their lives. Breaking this cycle requires intentional boundaries and a commitment to finding identity and worth in Christ alone.

4. Unhealthy Spiritual Intimacy ("You're the Only One Who Understands Me Spiritually")

Spiritual intimacy is a beautiful gift when shared within the context of a God-honoring relationship. However, when one person becomes the sole source of spiritual understanding or connection, it can lead to an unhealthy tie. Matthew 18:20 reminds us,

"For where two or three are gathered together in my name, there am I in the midst of them." Imagine someone saying, "You're the only one who understands me spiritually." While this may feel affirming, it places an undue burden on the relationship and can isolate both individuals from the broader spiritual community. Healthy spiritual intimacy involves shared growth within a community of believers, not exclusive reliance on one person.

A Love Worth Waiting: Hapily Ever After

5. Fantasy/Obsession, Even Through Social Media

In today's digital age, it's easy to form unhealthy attachments through social media. Constantly checking someone's profile, imagining scenarios, or obsessing over their life can create a soul tie that feels real but is entirely one-sided. Philippians 4:8 advises,

"Finally, brethren, whatsoever things are true, whatsoever things are honest, whatsoever things are just, whatsoever things are pure, whatsoever things are lovely, whatsoever things are of good report; if there be any virtue, and if there be any praise, think on these things." For example, someone might spend hours scrolling through a person's posts, building a fantasy relationship in their mind. This obsession not only distracts from real-life connections but also creates an emotional tie that can be difficult to break. Redirecting your focus to God's truth and engaging in meaningful, face-to-face relationships can help dismantle these unhealthy patterns.

Intimacy Without Boundaries: A Call to Guard Your Heart

Soul ties are not always formed by physical intimacy; they are often the result of emotional and spiritual connections that lack healthy boundaries. As Proverbs 3:5–6 encourages,

"Trust in the Lord with all thine heart; and lean not unto thine own understanding. In all thy ways acknowledge him, and he shall direct thy paths."

A Love Worth Waiting: Hapily Ever After

Ellen G. White also emphasizes the importance of guarding your heart, writing, *"The heart is the citadel of the soul. He who controls the heart controls the whole being."* By setting boundaries, seeking God's guidance, and involving trusted mentors, you can protect your heart and ensure that your relationships honor Him.

Soul ties formed without boundaries can hinder your emotional and spiritual growth. Whether through late-night talks, shared trauma, repetitive flirting, unhealthy spiritual intimacy, or social media obsession, these ties can create bonds that distract from God's purpose for your life. Recognizing these patterns and seeking God's healing is the first step toward freedom and restoration.

May this reflection inspire you to examine your relationships with wisdom and grace, trusting that God's love is the ultimate source of freedom and fulfillment.

God's Way: Holy Covenant, Holy Connection

God created emotional and sexual bonding to be **safe** within the covenant of marriage.

"Therefore shall a man leave his father and his mother, and shall cleave unto his wife: and they shall be one flesh." – Genesis 2:24

A Love Worth Waiting: Hapily Ever After

Outside that safety, even well-meaning connections can become binding cords that distort your ability to love freely in the future.

Breaking Unholy Soul Ties

Unholy soul ties are bonds that form when intimacy—emotional, spiritual, or otherwise—crosses God's intended boundaries. They can bind you to painful memories, unhealthy attachments, and even sin. Yet through the redeeming love of Christ, every chain can be broken. As Jesus declares in John 8:36,

"If the Son therefore shall make you free, ye shall be free indeed."

In the following steps, we explore a path toward freedom—a deliberate dismantling of unholy attachments through repentance, renunciation, decisive action, and rediscovering your identity in God.

1. Repent of the Connection

The first step in breaking an unholy soul tie is to honestly evaluate where your heart has wandered away from God's will. Acknowledge the bond that was formed in disobedience or misplaced intimacy. Repenting means confessing your transgressions to God, recognizing that this connection did not honor His design for relationships, and surrendering every remnant of that bond into His capable hands.

A Love Worth Waiting: Hapily Ever After

Consider the individual who repeatedly revisits memories that ought to be left in the past. In prayer, confess not only the sin of attachment but also the ways in which that connection has hindered your spiritual progress. As 1 John 1:9 assures us,

"If we confess our sins, he is faithful and just to forgive us our sins, and to cleanse us from all unrighteousness."

This act of repentance is like removing a damaged brick from a foundation so that new, God-ordained structure can emerge. Asking for God's forgiveness and healing lays the groundwork for freedom and renewal.

2. Renounce Emotional/Spiritual Claims

Once you have repented, formally renounce the emotional or spiritual claims that the unholy tie has over your life. In heartfelt prayer, declare that you no longer belong to that person or that past relationship — but solely to Christ. This renouncement is an act of spiritual defiance against the lingering claims of past attachments.

Imagine a person who, through repeated prayer, boldly proclaims, "I renounce this tie — I belong to Christ, and no longer will I allow any bond to hold me captive." This is a simple yet profound statement that serves the hold that the unhealthy connection has had over your spirit. In doing so, you affirm that your worth is now defined by Christ's love and not by past mistakes. Ellen G. White often reminds us that true freedom comes when we place our identity wholly in Christ, rather than in fleeting human attachments. This renunciation is both a spiritual declaration and a fresh start toward healing.

3. Remove Points of Access

Unholy soul ties often persist because we allow reminders of the past to remain in our daily lives. Removing points of access is a practical step with deep spiritual implications. These "access points" may be cellphone numbers, social media links, photographs, or gifts that continually stir up old memories and emotions.

Take, for example, a person who finds that every time they scroll through their social media feed, images, and messages resurrect old, unholy ties. Deciding to delete those contacts, block those profiles, or even discard tangible items can break the cycle of recurring pain. This physical act of removal symbolizes your commitment to guarding your heart—honoring Proverbs 4:23 :

"Keep thy heart with all diligence; for out of it are the issues of life."

By eliminating these triggers, you create a protected space for your healing to occur—a sanctuary that allows God's restorative power to work without interference.

4. Restore Your Identity in God

The final — and perhaps most transformative — step is to reclaim and restore your identity in God. Unholy soul ties leave a void that only God can fill. Replace the emptiness left by those unhealthy bonds with the rich truth of Scripture, the encouragement of godly friends, and divine affirmation.

Immerse yourself in the Word. Memorize verses that speak of your new identity in Christ, such as 2 Corinthians 5:17:

"Therefore if any man be in Christ, he is a new creature: old things are passed away; behold, all things are become new."

Invite regular fellowship with believers who can affirm and support you. Engage in activities that build up your spiritual life — a new hobby, serving in your church, or participating in group Bible studies. Ellen G. White once wrote, *"There is no higher calling than developing a character and identity that reflects the light of Christ."* In doing so, you replace the lingering shadows of past attachments with God's illuminating truth.

Breaking unholy soul ties is a process — a journey of repentance, renunciation, decisive removal of triggers, and the restoration of your God-ordained identity. These steps not only dismantle the unhealthy bonds that hold you captive but also pave the way for a life of freedom and purpose in Christ. Remember the promise of Jesus in John 8:36:

"If the Son therefore shall make you free, ye shall be free indeed."

May you find strength in His words, courage in His spirit, and renewed identity as you walk away from past chains into the liberating light of His eternal love.

May this reflection empower you to break free from unholy soul ties, restoring your heart and life in the grace and freedom offered by Christ.

Prayer to Break Soul Ties

Jesus, I give You every emotional bond that is not from You. I break, in Your name, every tie that has hindered my heart, clouded my mind, or grieved Your Spirit. Heal the parts of me still connected to people I no longer walk with. Replace those places with Your presence. I belong to You alone. Amen.

A Love Worth Waiting: Hapily Ever After

Reflection Questions

1. Have I formed unhealthy emotional or physical bonds in past relationships?

2. Is there someone I still feel connected to — even after we've separated?

3. What steps have I taken to break those ties in Jesus' name?

4. How can I build only godly, intentional soul ties moving forward?

Journal Prompt

Write a letter (you don't need to send it) to someone you feel tied to emotionally or spiritually. Pour out your heart, then pray a releasing prayer over it. End by writing a declaration: "I am tied to Christ, not to my past."

Chapter 9
The Art of Waiting: How God Prepares Hearts for Holy Love"

"But they that wait upon the Lord shall renew their strength; they shall mount up with wings as eagles; they shall run, and not be weary; and they shall walk, and not faint." – Isaiah 40:31

The Ache of the In-Between

Waiting is one of the hardest things to do when your heart is ready for love. You watch others find "their person." You pray. You journal. You cry. And still — silence.

You start to wonder:

- Is God late?
- Did I miss my chance?
- Is there something wrong with me?

But waiting isn't punishment. **Waiting is preparation.**

God does not waste a single second of your waiting season. In fact, it is in the waiting that He shapes you into the person who can carry the love He is preparing for you.

A Love Worth Waiting: Hapily Ever After

"To every thing there is a season, and a time to every purpose under the heaven." - Ecclesiastes 3:1

Story: From Delay to Destiny

Noemi was 32 and single. She had watched all her friends marry — some happily, others not. She served in church, grew in her career, traveled, and healed… but inside, she felt like time was slipping through her fingers.

Then she met Marcos — a widowed missionary with a quiet strength and deep heart for God. As they talked, she realized: *If we had met five years ago, I wouldn't have been ready. I would've sabotaged this.*

Looking back, the delay *wasn't denial*. It was grace. It was preparation.

God had been working on them both — so that when they met, they weren't just *ready for love*, they were *ready to give it the way God designed it*.

What Happens in the Waiting?

1. God Develops Your Character

"Knowing this, that the trying of your faith worketh patience." - James 1:3

A Love Worth Waiting: Hapily Ever After

Waiting is not passive — it's active surrender.

- God refines your identity so you don't look for it in a partner.
- He teaches you to love Him first — so you don't idolize your future spouse.
- He stretches your capacity to give — not just receive.

2. God Heals Your History

Occasionally God doesn't bring "the one" yet because He's still healing "the wounds" from the last one.

"He healeth the broken in heart, and bindeth up their wounds." - Psalm 147:3

Marriage should be entered with clarity, not confusion; wholeness, not desperation.

Healing now protects your love later.

3. God Trains You in Purpose

"Delight thyself also in the Lord; and he shall give thee the desires of thine heart." - Psalm 37:4

Many people waste their single years waiting to be chosen — instead of walking in their calling.

A Love Worth Waiting: Hapily Ever After

When your life is full of purpose, love will not distract you from your mission — it will enhance it.

Did You Know?

Psychologists agree that individuals who develop strong self-identity and life purpose before entering romantic relationships experience **healthier attachment**, greater satisfaction, and less emotional dependence.

Spiritual maturity, emotional health, and a clear sense of purpose are some of the **strongest predictors of long-term marital success**. — Source: Dr. Sue Johnson, Love Sense: The Revolutionary New Science of Romantic Relationships

God Is Not Late — He's Precise

This meditation invites you to embrace the truth that our God orchestrates life through divine appointments. His timing is never accidental or delayed; instead, it is custom-tailored to our growth, readiness, and His eternal purpose. As you consider the examples of divine timing in Scripture, may you find encouragement and a renewed trust in God's perfect plan.

A Love Worth Waiting: Hapily Ever After

Divine Appointments That Speak of Precision

God's track record for divine timing is evident throughout Scripture. He orchestrates life's milestones with remarkable precision:

- **He brought Eve to Adam only when Adam was ready to receive her.** God did not rush the process of creation but arranged their union according to the readiness of Adam's heart—a divine appointment that was both deliberate and sacred.

- **He kept Isaac single until Rebekah arrived at the well.** In the story of Isaac, God patiently guarded the promise of a suitable partner. Isaac's solitude was not a sign of neglect but an intentional period of preparation until the right match appeared at the perfect moment.

- **He trained Ruth through loss before bringing Boaz into her life.** Ruth's journey is a testimony to God's refining process. Through her hardships and losses, God prepared her character for a profound covenant union with Boaz—a relationship that would ultimately reveal His redemptive plan for a nation.

In each of these examples, love and redemption were not hurried. Instead, God's precision ensured that every appointment aligned with His higher purposes of shaping character, deepening faith, and manifesting His glory.

A Love Worth Waiting: Hapily Ever After

The Call to Wait on the Lord

The Scriptures offer a timeless invitation to trust in God's timing. As Psalm 27:14 exhorts: "Wait on the Lord: be of good courage, and he shall strengthen thine heart: wait, I say, on the Lord."

This verse reminds us that waiting is not a passive state but an act of courageous trust. When we refuse to yield to impatience, we allow God's spirit to work in us, molding our character, and preparing us for the blessings that are inseparable from obedience and perseverance.

Remember: Waiting doesn't delay your blessing — **impatience does.** In our haste, we risk compromising the very process through which God refines us. When we choose to rest in His promise and timing, every season of waiting becomes a sacred period of deepening trust and preparation for the future.

Embracing God's Precise Timing in Your Life

Consider these reflective questions as you evaluate your journey of faith and relationships:

- **Are you patiently trusting God's timing in your life?** Like Adam waiting to receive his companion, are you prepared to welcome God's appointed people, opportunities, and seasons into your life when they come?

A Love Worth Waiting: Hapily Ever After

- **Do you see the beauty in divine appointments rather than rushing ahead of His plan?** Recognize that each delay or season of waiting is a setup for a greater blessing—each moment finely tuned to your growth and God's purpose.

- **How might impatience be hindering your progress?** Reflect on the ways impulsiveness or hurried decisions might be detracting from the careful preparation God desires for your life's journey.

When you look to God's blueprint for love and life, you find assurance that nothing is truly random. Every detail, every pause, is part of His masterful design—a reminder that God is never late; He is always precise.

God Is Not Late — He's Precise. In His divine appointments, He orchestrates every detail of your journey. From bringing Eve to Adam, keeping Isaac waiting until Rebekah appeared, or refining Ruth's character through loss before uniting her with Boaz, His timing is intentional. Trusting in God means embracing the sacred waiting, knowing that when you do, you align yourself with a destiny deliberately and lovingly designed by the Creator.

May you continue to wait on the Lord with courage and anticipation, confident that every season of delay in your life is a testimony to God's precise, perfect timing.

A Love Worth Waiting: Hapily Ever After

May this reflection inspire you to trust in God's perfect timing and to delight in the precise, intentional appointments He has designed for your life.

Prayer for the Waiting Season

Here are some reflective meditation and prayer on the waiting season — one that invites faith over frustration, restores hope over desperation, and aligns your every step with God's perfect timing. As you read, may you be encouraged to see this season not as a void or delay but as a fertile ground in which God is preparing you for the blessings He has already arranged.

Prayer for the Waiting Season

Lord, teach me to wait with faith, not frustration. In the stillness of waiting, our natural urge is to feel impatient or restless. Yet Scripture reminds us that waiting is a sacred opportunity to grow and be molded in Your image. As Psalm 27:14 exhorts, "Wait on the LORD: be of good courage, and he shall strengthen thine heart; wait, I say, on the LORD." When frustration threatens to take root, let us remember that the season of waiting is a season of preparation. Just as a seed lies dormant in darkness before bursting forth into bloom, our lives too are being nurtured by Your divine hand. Reflect on moments when delays turned into breakthroughs — all testimonies of Your faithfulness and timing.

A Love Worth Waiting: Hapily Ever After

Remind me that You are never late. In our hurried world, it is easy to equate delay with neglect. Yet, Your Word assures us that Your timing is perfect. Isaiah 55:8-9 declares, "For my thoughts are not your thoughts, neither are your ways my ways, saith the LORD."

When doubt creeps into our hearts, may we recall that the Creator of all things works outside the limitations of human time. Picture a runner in a race: the finish line is reached not by rushing but by a steady, confident pace. In the waiting season, let us emulate that runner—trusting that in Your perfect schedule, every moment is neither early nor late but exactly as it should be.

Fill my heart with purpose, healing, and joy — not desperation. Waiting can become a time of longing when we focus on what is missing. Instead, may this season be marked by the deep, sustaining joy that comes from knowing You. Psalm 147:3 comforts us with these words:

"He healeth the broken in heart, and bindeth up their wounds." As you wait, allow Your Word to renew your spirit and fill you with hope. Consider the example of a person recovering from loss—each day spent in prayer and quiet reflection slowly repairs the fractures of despair, replacing them with healing grace and divine purpose. Let love and gratitude be the language of your heart as You restore wholeness from within.

A Love Worth Waiting: Hapily Ever After

And when the time is right, align my steps with the one You have prepared. The journey of waiting finds its fulfillment when we surrender ourselves wholly to Your guidance. Proverbs 3:5-6 instructs us to: "Trust in the LORD with all thine heart; and lean not unto thine own understanding. In all thy ways acknowledge him, and he shall direct thy paths."

Envision a traveler navigating unknown territory — their eyes fixed on the path revealed by a trusted guide. In the fullness of time, may every step be aligned with the destiny You have orchestrated so that every choice reflects Your will. Let the waiting season refine your vision and illuminate the way ahead, transforming uncertainty into a confident walk of faith.

Until then, make me whole in You. Amen.

Complete the prayer by asking God to fill every emptiness with His presence. It is in Your wholeness that we find our true identity. As Ellen G. White beautifully reminds us, *"When we have learned to wait upon the Lord, our souls are filled with His abiding peace, and no earthly trial can shake the foundation He has laid within us."* In this sacred waiting, may Your love be the balm that perfects us, making us vessels of hope and channels of Your divine grace.

The waiting season is not merely a pause between events but a divine appointment with God. It is a time to cultivate faith over frustration, to remember that You

A Love Worth Waiting: Hapily Ever After

are never late, and to allow Your healing presence to fill our hearts with purpose and joy. As you journey through this season, lean on the promises of Scripture, seek encouragement in godly fellowship, and hold fast to the assurance that every step is aligned with Your eternal plan.

May this prayer and reflection serve as a constant reminder that Your waiting is not wasted but wonderfully orchestrated by God's perfect hand. Stay rooted in His love, and trust that the season of waiting is crafting a destiny far beyond your present understanding. Amen.

A Love Worth Waiting: Hapily Ever After

Reflection Questions

1. Am I waiting actively — growing in purpose, identity, and healing?

2. Have I surrendered the *timing* and the *person* to God?

3. Am I preparing to give love, not just receive it?

4. What part of my heart still needs healing before marriage?

Journal Prompt

Write a letter to your future spouse. Don't just express longing — express who you are becoming while you wait. Then write a letter to yourself, affirming the value and beauty of your current season.

Chapter 10
True Love Waits: Purity, Power, and the Purpose of Saving Yourself

"Flee fornication. Every sin that a man doeth is without the body; but he that committeth fornication sinneth against his own body." – 1 Corinthians 6:18

What the World Calls Power, God Calls Poison

The world calls it empowerment. TV shows say "explore yourself." Social media says "you only live once." But God says: *"Wait."*

Not because He wants to deprive you — but because He longs to protect you.

Purity is not shame. It is power. It is the bold, radical declaration: *"I will not give away what God designed to be holy."*

"Satan seeks to lower the standard of purity and to weaken the character by corrupting the thoughts and inflaming the passions. Those who would preserve their powers for the service of God must avoid the excitement of impurity." — Ellen G. White, Messages to Young People, p. 460

A Love Worth Waiting: Hapily Ever After

This chapter is not about guilt. It's about freedom — whether you're still walking in purity, or longing to return to it. God can redeem and restore what was lost, and guard what remains.

Story: A Different Kind of Courage

David grew up in a home where abstinence was expected. But in college, everything changed. His friends mocked his convictions. "Bro, you're too holy for your own good."

He doubted himself. Almost gave in. But one night, after a powerful message on purity and purpose, he made a new vow: *"I will wait — not because I'm better, but because I'm God's."*

Years later, at his wedding, he stood with tears in his eyes as his bride said: "Thank you… for guarding what most guys would have traded for a moment of pleasure. You saved it for me."

It was worth it.

Why Purity Still Matters

1. Your Body is a Temple

"Know ye not that your body is the temple of the Holy Ghost which is in you… and ye are not your own?" - 1 Corinthians 6:19, KJV

A Love Worth Waiting: Hapily Ever After

You don't need a wedding to be sacred. Your purity makes you a dwelling place for God Himself.

You are not common. You are not cheap. You are **consecrated**.

2. Sex Was Never Just Physical

Hollywood says it's just a physical act. But science — and Scripture — say otherwise.

Sex creates **emotional, chemical, and spiritual bonds** designed to knit two souls into one.

"The two shall become one flesh." – Genesis 2:24

Outside of covenant, that bond creates pain instead of unity.

3. Purity Protects Your Future Marriage

Every past sexual encounter becomes a *memory in your marriage bed* — unless surrendered and healed.

Couples who choose abstinence before marriage report higher trust, deeper emotional intimacy, and lower divorce rates.

"True love will not lead to the ruin of one whom he professes to love. It will not degrade, it will not defile, it will not ruin." — Messages to Young People, p. 446

A Love Worth Waiting: Hapily Ever After

Purity is not just about saying "no" — it's about saying *yes* to something better.

4. You Can Begin Again

If you've already crossed the line — there is no condemnation. Only invitation.

Invitation to forgiveness. To healing. To restoration.

Jesus said to the woman caught in adultery: *"Neither do I condemn thee: go, and sin no more."* (John 8:11)

You are not your past. You are His beloved.

Did You Know?

A longitudinal study by the Institute for Family Studies found that individuals who abstained from premarital sex — or who renewed a commitment to purity later in life — reported significantly higher marital satisfaction, trust, and emotional bonding.

Purity is not outdated. It's divine design. — Source: Wilcox & Wolfinger, 2019, IFS

How to Guard Your Purity (or Begin Again)

This guide is designed to help you reaffirm your commitment to living a life that honors God through clear boundaries, godly community, purposeful living, confession, and daily prayer. May you find encouragement and strength as you embrace a renewed path of purity and wholeness in Christ.

1. Set Physical Boundaries Before Emotion Takes Over

Before passion gains free rein, decide on clear physical boundaries that honor the sacredness of your body. Just as a builder marks the limits of a foundation before constructing a lasting home, you must intentionally determine your limits while you are still in full control—not in the heat of the moment. Our bodies are temples of the Holy Spirit, and by setting boundaries proactively, you're protecting that temple from being tarnished by impulsive actions. Reflect on 1 Corinthians 6:19-20 :

"What? know ye not that your body is the temple of the Holy Ghost which is in you, which ye have of God, and ye are not your own? For ye are bought with a price: therefore glorify God in your body."

For example, if you're entering a new relationship, it can be wise to discuss and agree on your boundaries ahead of time. This proactive strategy ensures that both of you honor God's design for intimacy—even before emotions run high.

2. Surround Yourself with People Who Share Your Values

Purity is rarely maintained in isolation. It thrives within a community of supportive, like-minded believers—a true purity circle that encourages you to live according to godly standards. Proverbs 27:17 reminds us:

"Iron sharpeneth iron; so a man sharpeneth the countenance of his friend."

Seek friends, mentors, and church communities that reinforce your values rather than pressure you toward compromise. Imagine a circle of trusted companions who meet regularly for Bible study, prayer, and honest discussion. This type of community helps keep you accountable and strengthens your resolve to maintain purity in every area of your life.

3. Replace Temptation with Mission

When temptation tries to draw you away from your commitment, let your heart be refreshed by a higher calling. Fill your days with purpose and mission so that the allure of momentary pleasure dims in comparison to the passionate pursuit of God's will. Romans 12:2 advises:

"And be not conformed to this world: but be ye transformed by the renewing of your mind, that ye may prove what is that good, and acceptable, and perfect, will of God."

A Love Worth Waiting: Hapily Ever After

Consider redirecting your focus: rather than lingering on temptation, invest time in serving at your church, volunteering in your community, or pursuing activities that glorify God. When you burn for His mission, you will naturally find less room for any compromise that detracts from your heavenly calling.

4. Confess and Receive Healing If You've Fallen

Even when you stumble, God's grace extends beyond mere forgiveness—He restores your dignity and renews your spirit. Confession is not an admission of defeat but a brave step toward freedom. When you confess your shortcomings and sins to God, you open yourself to His redemptive healing. 1 John 1:9 promises:

"If we confess our sins, he is faithful and just to forgive us our sins, and to cleanse us from all unrighteousness."

Embrace the truth that God doesn't just forgive; He heals. Whether through private prayer, accountable conversations with a trusted mentor, or supportive counseling, allow His love to restore you. As Ellen G. White reminds us, true restoration brings back the dignity and brightness of a life dedicated to His service, preparing you to begin again with a renewed heart.

5. Pray Daily for Purity of Heart, Mind, and Body

True purity is cultivated from the inside out, beginning with the heart and mind. Daily prayer is a powerful practice that reorients your thoughts and desires toward God. Psalm 51:10 (KJV) echoes this need:

"Create in me a clean heart, O God; and renew a right spirit within me."

Make it a daily habit to ask the Lord for purity. Before the challenges of the day take hold, spend time in prayer—whether in the quiet of the morning or during moments of pause throughout your day. This spiritual discipline guards your mind against negative influences and builds a life where every action reflects your commitment to God. Over time, this practice transforms purity from a fleeting goal into a way of life.

Guarding your purity is a purposeful, daily journey—a commitment that begins with setting proactive physical boundaries, seeking a community that shares your values, redirecting temptation through a clear mission, and embracing God's healing grace through confession. Coupled with daily prayer, these steps will help you begin again, living a life that honors God in every thought, word, and deed.

May this comprehensive guide empower you to guard your purity and to begin again with confidence in God's redemptive love, knowing that each step taken is a deliberate act of worship and a reflection of your commitment to His eternal design.

A Love Worth Waiting: Hapily Ever After

Prayer for Purity

Jesus, I give You my body, my emotions, my desires. Guard what is sacred. Cleanse what is wounded. Heal what I gave away. I don't want to be pure just in action — but in heart. Teach me how to wait with joy, and love with holiness. I belong to You. Amen.

Reflection Questions

1. Do I see purity as a burden — or as protection and purpose?

2. What boundaries do I need to put in place today?

3. Have I allowed shame to keep me from God's grace?

4. What kind of legacy do I want to bring into my future marriage?

Journal Prompt

Write a purity pledge — not one based on fear or religion, but on **love**. A vow to God that you desire to walk in wholeness, healing, and holiness — from this day forward, no matter your past.

A Love Worth Waiting: Hapily Ever After

Chapter 11
God-Written Love Stories: What Happens When You Let Him Choose

God-Written Love Stories: What Happens When You Let Him Choose

"The steps of a good man are ordered by the Lord: and he delighteth in his way." – Psalm 37:23

Stories Only Heaven Can Write

She prayed for him before she ever met him. He asked God for a sign, and peace became his answer. It wasn't a fairy tale. It was something better: **a story written by God**.

In today's world, everyone wants to write their love story:

- Swipe fast.
- Love intensely.
- Leave when it hurts.
- Repeat the cycle.

A Love Worth Waiting: Hapily Ever After

But God doesn't write throwaway romances. He writes **eternal covenants**. He doesn't improvise. He **orders steps**. He doesn't rush you off a cliff — He prepares you to fly.

"In the choice of a life companion, let the youth be guided by principle. Let them seek counsel from those who have experience, and above all, let them make this a matter of earnest prayer." — Ellen G. White, Messages to Young People, p. 445

Story: When God Holds the Pen

Camila stopped searching. After multiple heartbreaks, she prayed: "Lord, I don't want pain dressed up as love anymore. If You're not writing this story, I don't want to write even the first chapter."

During a mission trip to the Amazon, she met David. It wasn't love at first sight. It was friendship, service, prayer... and time.

Two years later, standing under a simple altar, Camila whispered through tears: "*Thank you... for waiting on the script God was writing.*"

There was no drama. No doubts. Just peace. Because when God writes the story, **peace signs every page**.

A Love Worth Waiting: Hapily Ever After

5 Signs of a God-Written Love Story

When God Himself writes your love story, it bears fruit in every area of your relationship—from peace and shared purpose to community, integrity, and character. May these signs inspire you to recognize His divine touch in your union and guide you toward a relationship that honors Him and reflects His love to the world.

1. Consistent Peace from the Holy Spirit

A God-written love story is marked by a calm assurance that comes not from human logic but from the peace of the Holy Spirit. As Colossians 3:15 declares,

"And let the peace of God rule in your hearts..."

This peace is not noisy or flamboyant; it is subtle and constant. When you experience consistent peace, you know that God's Spirit is at work—even amidst life's storms. For example, consider moments when disagreements or challenges arise: instead of turmoil or frustration, both partners find calm assurance in prayer and reflection. That inner tranquility, a gentle yet profound confirmation of God's presence, tells you that your relationship is anchored in divine truth. When His peace is present, confusion, torment, or undue pressure simply do not have room to flourish.

A Love Worth Waiting: Hapily Ever After

2. You Both Love God More Than You Love Each Other

In a God-centered relationship, God's love is the primary focus, and the affection you share reflects His glory rather than competing with it. As Amos 3:3 asks, "Can two walk together, except they be agreed?"

This sign means that both partners pursue a deep, personal relationship with God that sets the foundation for every other connection. When each person values God above all—including their romantic love—every interaction becomes an extension of their devotion to Him. Consider a couple who diligently prays together, engages in regular Bible study, and involves God in every decision. Their love for one another flourishes only because it is a reflection of their gratitude and commitment to the One who first loved them. Conversely, if one partner seeks Christ while the other drifts, the dissonance reveals a divided path, not a truly divine alignment.

3. There Is Shared Purpose, Not Just Attraction

God does not pair people merely for romantic attraction—He brings them together for a higher mission. A God-written love story is defined by a shared vision that goes beyond physical attraction. As noted in *The Adventist Home* (p. 35),

"God designs that homes shall be missionary fields."

A Love Worth Waiting: Hapily Ever After

This means that your relationship is not just about the thrills of attraction but about undertaking a purposeful mission together. Imagine a couple who isn't satisfied with simply enjoying each other's company on a superficial level, but who also seeks to reach out in service to others—whether it be through community outreach, church ministries, or compassionate acts that reflect the love of Christ. Their union serves as a beacon of hope, a living testimony that relationships grounded in divine purpose can transform not only their lives but also the lives of those around them.

4. The Relationship Welcomes Counsel and Community

A relationship written by God is open to the light and nurtured by wise counsel and supportive community. It does not hide behind closed doors but welcomes the insights of mentors, parents, and spiritual leaders. Proverbs 11:14 reminds us,

"In the multitude of counsellors there is safety."

This sign indicates that you are not isolated in your journey of love. Instead, you invite those who are mature in their faith to speak truth into your relationship. For instance, consider a couple who regularly attends couples' meetings or participates in community Bible studies; these gatherings offer guidance, affirmation, and a sense of accountability. The counsel of trusted advisors helps to confirm that the love you share is not only tender but also rooted in wisdom and discernment—a vital safeguard against the inevitable challenges of life.

5. Both Partners Display the Fruits of the Spirit

The ultimate evidence of a God-written love story is seen in the character of the individuals involved. Matthew 7:20 teaches,

"Wherefore by their fruits ye shall know them."

When both partners exhibit the fruits of the Spirit—kindness, patience, self-control, faithfulness, and love—it is a clear sign that the relationship is grounded in Christ. This goes far beyond physical chemistry or superficial charm. It speaks to the transformation that takes place when hearts are surrendered to the Lord. Picture a couple who actively chooses forgiveness over anger, encouragement over criticism, and service over self-interest. Their actions mirror the love of Christ in such a way that others can see His handiwork in their lives. It is a testament to the fact that a relationship built on spiritual maturity is both resilient and radiant.

A God-written love story stands out by its depth and divine alignment. It carries a quiet, persistent peace, reflects a mutual love for God above all, and is fueled by a shared mission that goes far beyond attraction. It welcomes wise counsel and is ultimately marked by the fruits of the Spirit—evidence that these hearts beat in unison with God's eternal design. As you consider these signs, may you be encouraged to seek a love that

A Love Worth Waiting: Hapily Ever After

is not merely human but has been written by God Himself.

May these reflections illuminate your path, confirming that your love story is divinely orchestrated—a testament to the transformative and enduring power of God's love.

Did You Know?

Research from Baylor University and the University of Chicago shows that **marriages formed through active spiritual communities** (such as church or missions) experience higher satisfaction, lower abuse rates, and greater longevity than secular dating patterns.

God really does write the best stories. — Source: Wilcox, W. B. (2017), *National Marriage Project*

When God Chooses, He Also Sustains

When God unites hearts, He also provides:

- Grace to wait
- Wisdom to discern
- Strength to commit

A Love Worth Waiting: Hapily Ever After

"What therefore God hath joined together, let not man put asunder." – Mark 10:9

Prayer

Lord, if You are not writing my story, I don't want to pick up the pen. Slow my heart down. Clear my mind. Let my emotions not outpace Your voice. I trust You to write something better than I could ever imagine. When You write it, it won't just feel good — it will glorify You. Amen.

Reflection Questions

1. Am I letting God write my love story — or trying to control the plot?

2. What qualities would I look for in someone if my top priority was pleasing God?

3. How do I respond when God says, "not yet"?

4. Am I spiritually ready to love someone like Jesus does?

A Love Worth Waiting: Hapily Ever After

🖐 Journal Prompt

Write a letter to your future self on your wedding day. What do you hope you'll be thanking God for? What are you praying your story will say? What kind of love are you asking Him to write for you?

A Love Worth Waiting: Hapily Ever After

Chapter 12
Before You Say Yes: Questions You Must Ask Before You Marry

"Through wisdom is an house builded; and by understanding it is established: And by knowledge shall the chambers be filled with all precious and pleasant riches." – Proverbs 24:3–4

Love Isn't Enough

"I'm in love." "But he's a good man." She's beautiful, and we've been together for years."

These are common reasons people say yes to marriage — and also common reasons they later say, *"I made a mistake."*

Marriage isn't built on butterflies. It's built on **wisdom, clarity,** and **alignment**. Love is essential — but **it must be examined.**

Before you say *yes* to forever, God invites you to ask the deep questions — not just about your partner, but about yourself.

Because the *right person at the wrong time* is still the wrong decision.

A Love Worth Waiting: Hapily Ever After

"It is a life-long decision. Too much importance cannot be placed upon the selection of a companion for life."
— Ellen G. White, Messages to Young People, p. 435

Story: Questions She Never Asked

Nina said yes because she didn't want to lose him. She never asked about finances, faith, childhood wounds, or conflict resolution. They prayed, but never went deep. She thought, *"We'll figure it out once we're married."*

Three years later, they were more like roommates than partners. He refused counseling. She resented his passivity. They loved each other — but didn't *understand* each other.

They didn't ask the hard questions — and now they lived in silent disappointment.

10 Questions to Ask Before You Say Yes

1. Is this person bringing me closer to God — or distracting me from Him?

"Seek ye first the kingdom of God..." – Matthew 6:33

A Love Worth Waiting: Hapily Ever After

Marriage multiplies the direction you're already going. If they're not pursuing Christ now, they won't suddenly prioritize Him later.

2. Do we have compatible visions and missions in life?

God doesn't only unite hearts — He unites callings.

"How can two walk together, except they be agreed?" – Amos 3:3

Do you share goals, values, and a passion for building something beyond yourselves?

3. How do they handle anger, pressure, and failure?

You're not marrying their best self on a good day. You're committing to them in moments of stress, loss, and conflict.

"A fool uttereth all his mind: but a wise man keepeth it in till afterwards." – Proverbs 29:11

Watch how they respond when life squeezes them — that's what will show up in your home.

4. Are they willing to grow, apologize, and be corrected?

No one is perfect. But someone who is **teachable** is someone who can build a lasting marriage.

"He that refuseth instruction despiseth his own soul: but he that heareth reproof getteth understanding." - Proverbs 15:32

Stubbornness before marriage becomes destruction after marriage.

5. Do we communicate well — or avoid real conversations?

Do you feel heard, seen, and respected? Can you both talk about finances, sexual expectations, family, and faith without shame or shutdown?

Poor communication is the seed of future disconnection.

6. Have we seen each other in every season — joy, grief, stress, conflict?

Attraction is easy in springtime. But covenant must survive all seasons.

If you've never walked through hardship together, you may not yet know their true character.

7. Are our families and spiritual mentors supportive — or sounding alarms?

"In the multitude of counsellors there is safety." - Proverbs 11:14

Don't ignore red flags your loved ones raise. Wise counsel is God's safeguard.

8. Have we healed from past wounds — or are we bringing baggage into marriage?

You don't need to be perfect — but you need to be **aware** and **committed to growth**.

"He healeth the broken in heart..." - Psalm 147:3

Unhealed wounds will bleed into your marriage. Love demands preparation, not just passion.

9. Are we equally yoked spiritually?

You don't need to be at the same "level," but you do need the **same Lord**.

"Be ye not unequally yoked together with unbelievers..." - 2 Corinthians 6:14

Spiritual mismatch creates a lifetime of silent battle.

A Love Worth Waiting: Hapily Ever After

10. What does God say? Have I prayed — and waited — for His peace?

No answer is complete until Heaven has spoken.

God's voice may not come with lightning — but His peace will stay through every storm.

"Thou wilt keep him in perfect peace, whose mind is stayed on thee." – Isaiah 26:3

Did You Know?

Couples who go through **premarital counseling** reduce their risk of divorce by **31%**, according to the Journal of Family Psychology.

Asking intentional questions **before** the altar leads to deeper satisfaction **after** it. — Source: Stanley, S. M. et al. (2006). Premarital Education and Relationship Quality.

Prayer for Discernment

Lord, don't let me say yes out of fear, pressure, or fantasy. Give me eyes to see as You see. Give me courage to walk away if it's not from You. And if it is, give me peace, wisdom, and joy. Lead my heart with truth — not just emotion. Amen.

A Love Worth Waiting: Hapily Ever After

Reflection Questions

1. What questions have I avoided asking — out of fear of the answer?

2. Have I invited God and wise counsel into my relationship journey?

3. Am I emotionally and spiritually ready to say "yes" to a covenant?

4. What do I believe marriage is — and what do I still need to learn?

📝 Journal Prompt

Write out your own personalized list of 5–10 questions you believe God is prompting you to ask in your season of preparation. Then write a prayer asking Him to give you courage, clarity, and the peace to wait until the answer is clear.

A Love Worth Waiting: Hapily Ever After

Chapter 13
Love After Yes: What to Expect and How to Prepare for Engagement

"Commit thy way unto the Lord; trust also in him; and he shall bring it to pass." – Psalm 37:5, KJV

The Yes Is Only the Beginning

You said yes. The ring is on. The countdown begins. The excitement is real. But so are the questions. Will we be ready? What if fears creep in? What does God expect now?

Too many people focus on the *wedding* and forget about the *marriage*. But engagement is not just a romantic interlude. It is a **sacred window of preparation** — a refining season, a time of spiritual and emotional strengthening.

God didn't design engagement to be a waiting room for pleasure or stress — He designed it to be a **workshop for covenant**.

"The formation of a happy union depends upon the cultivation of mind and heart. Let each seek to make the other's life happy." — Ellen G. White, The Adventist Home, p. 103

A Love Worth Waiting: Hapily Ever After

Story: The Test Before the Vow

Emma and Gabriel had been dating for three years. Their engagement brought so much joy — but also unexpected tension. Finances. Communication styles. Pressure from family. For a moment, Emma wondered, *"Are we failing already?"*

But wise counsel reminded them: *Engagement is not about being perfect — it's about preparing with God.* They started premarital counseling, fasted weekly, and committed to honesty and humility. By their wedding day, they weren't just "in love" — they were ready for war and worship, together.

7 Things to Expect During Engagement — and How to Prepare

Here are some reflective exploration of the key challenges and opportunities during the engagement season—a time marked by intense emotions, spiritual battles, and the laying of a firm foundation for a God-centered union. May these insights encourage you to navigate each season with prayer, wise counsel, and a heart grounded in the everlasting truth of God's Word.

1. Emotional Whirlwinds

Engagement is a season where joy and nerves often interlace; the excitement of future promises can sometimes stir up anxieties as well. What matters most is not the complete elimination of these emotions, but anchoring them in truth. As Psalm 112:7 proclaims, "He shall not be afraid of evil tidings: his heart is fixed, trusting in the Lord."

Embrace these emotional whirlwinds as a normal part of your journey by setting aside dedicated, weekly moments to pray and discuss your fears together. In doing so, you allow God to steady your hearts, replacing unpredictable stormy feelings with a sure, unwavering peace that comes only when trust in the Lord is fully embraced. A couple who intentionally communicates can turn even the most turbulent feelings into opportunities for spiritual growth and intimacy.

2. Spiritual Battles

When God ordains a relationship, the enemy does not sit idly by. Increased temptations, distractions, doubts, and delays can arise as spiritual battles to thwart divine plans. Ephesians 6:12 reminds us,

"For we wrestle not against flesh and blood, but against principalities, against powers, against the rulers of the darkness of this world, against spiritual wickedness in high places."

Understanding that these battles are not a reflection of personal inadequacies but part of the spiritual warfare that accompanies all God-ordained endeavors allows you to respond with prayer and unity. Arm yourselves together by fasting, praying, and inviting trusted friends and mentors to pray over your relationship. By doing so, you counteract the enemy's schemes and fortify your bond as you walk in the victory set forth by Christ.

3. Premarital Counseling

Premarital counseling is non-negotiable—not a sign of weakness but a profound mark of maturity. It provides a structured opportunity to explore the critical dimensions of your future life together. In these sessions, delve into areas such as:

- Finances
- Family dynamics
- Sex and expectations
- Spiritual leadership
- Conflict resolution
- Children and parenting

The wisdom of Proverbs 15:22 declares, "Plans fail for lack of counsel, but with many advisers they succeed."

A Love Worth Waiting: Hapily Ever After

Through premarital counseling, you create a solid foundation upon which every future challenge can be met with unity and understanding. This process equips you with practical strategies and deepens your spiritual connection, ensuring that the plans and vision for your marriage are aligned with God's will.

4. Revisiting Boundaries

As emotional intimacy deepens during engagement, so does the temptation to blur physical boundaries. It is essential to revisit and renew your purity commitments regularly. Jesus' words in Matthew 26:41 offer powerful guidance for this season: "Watch and pray, that ye enter not into temptation: the spirit is indeed willing, but the flesh is weak."

By consciously assessing and strengthening boundaries—a process that might include enlisting accountability partners—you ensure that your love remains patient and undiluted by momentary passions. Consistently returning to these boundaries helps keep your focus on building a relationship that honors God above all else, reinforcing that true love is willing to wait for the fullness of what God has destined for you.

5. Pressure from People

During engagement, well-intentioned opinions from family, friends, or even church members may emerge.

However, remember that your engagement is not a committee decision—it is a covenant made between you, your partner, and God. Romans 14:5 advises, "Let every man be fully persuaded in his own mind."

Instead of allowing external voices to dictate your course, seek godly counsel from trusted mentors who speak the truth in love. Always come back to the divine peace that only the Lord can bring. Balancing outside influence with your personal convictions ensures that your decisions are reflective of God's will rather than simply conforming to popular opinion.

6. Deepened Communication

Engagement presents the unique opportunity to master the art of communication. True success in any marriage is often rooted in how effectively couples learn to listen, express themselves honestly, and resolve disagreements gracefully. James 1:19 encourages us to,

"Let every man be swift to hear, slow to speak, slow to wrath."

Developing deep, honest communication during this season strengthens your current relationship and lays the groundwork for how you'll resolve future conflicts. The way you speak now is a predictor of how you will continue to interact throughout life. Embrace this time to refine your communication skills, ensuring that both love and respect are at the heart of every conversation.

7. Vision Building

Engagement is far more than planning a wedding or setting a seating chart—it is about cultivating a shared covenant vision for your future. Ask yourselves critical questions such as:

- What will our prayer life look like?
- How will we serve God together?
- What kind of home do we want to build?

Habakkuk 2:2 instructs, "Write the vision, and make it plain upon tables, that he may run that readeth it."

By engaging in purposeful vision building, you align your hearts and goals with God's eternal plan. This exercise deepens your spiritual bond, ensuring that every aspect of your future—from everyday routines to major life decisions—is infused with a sense of divine mission and mutual commitment.

The engagement season is a multifaceted journey characterized by emotional highs and challenges, spiritual battles, the invaluable process of premarital counseling, the continuous need to revisit boundaries, navigating external pressures, deepening communication, and building a visionary foundation. Each of these areas, when approached with prayer, wise counsel, and a heart fixed on Scripture, creates a robust framework for a marriage that truly honors God. Embrace these principles as stepping stones toward a relationship that not only thrives in the present but is also anchored in eternal truths.

May this comprehensive guide serve as both a reminder and a roadmap, empowering you to navigate your engagement with wisdom, unity, and an unshakable reliance on God's perfect plan.

Did You Know?

A *Psychology Today* study found that couples who had clear spiritual, financial, and family planning discussions during engagement reported higher long-term satisfaction, even five years into marriage.

Those who ignored hard conversations reported significantly **higher regret** — especially in areas like sex, money, and in-law conflict.

Prayer for Engagement

Lord, now that we've said yes, teach us how to *prepare for the vow*. Guard our hearts from distraction. Purify our desires. Refine our vision. Build us into a covenant-ready couple — not just for the altar, but for the mission ahead. Amen.

A Love Worth Waiting: Hapily Ever After

Reflection Questions

1. Am I preparing for the *marriage* — or just the *wedding*?

2. What are the spiritual and emotional areas I still need to grow in?

3. Are we avoiding any important conversations out of fear?

4. How can we make engagement a season of worship — not just work?

📝 Journal Prompt

Write a letter to your fiancé(e) expressing what you hope this engagement will build between you. Share your prayer for the kind of love, grace, and strength you desire to carry into your marriage.

A Love Worth Waiting: Hapily Ever After

Chapter 14
Marriage on Mission: What Happens When Two Become One in Christ

"And they twain shall be one flesh: so then they are no more twain, but one flesh." – Mark 10:8, KJV

Not Just Love — A Legacy

Marriage is not just about happiness. It's about **impact**. It's about what two people, surrendered to Christ, can do **together** for the Kingdom.

When God brings two lives together, it's never just for romance — it's for **mission**. A godly marriage is not a retirement plan — it's a **battle station**. A place where love heals, discipleship flows, children are shaped, and light shines into darkness.

"Marriage is something that will influence and affect your life both in this world and in the world to come."
— Ellen G. White, Messages to Young People, p. 435

A marriage on mission doesn't just survive — it shakes nations, blesses generations, and multiplies heaven's influence on earth.

A Love Worth Waiting: Hapily Ever After

Story: When Two Became a Ministry

Samuel and Tania got married after serving together in youth ministry. From day one, they committed to pray every morning, host a Bible study weekly, and always ask, *"What can we do for the Lord together?"*

In ten years, they've helped plant two churches, mentored dozens of couples, and raised three children who know their home is a place of faith and love.

Their secret?

"We don't just love each other," Tania said, "we love God *more together* than we ever did apart."

5 Truths About Kingdom Marriages

According to Bible.com, A Kingdom marriage is defined as - a covenantal union where a man and woman commit to function under God's authority, aiming to reflect God's image and expand His kingdom on Earth. It's not just about personal happiness but about advancing God's purpose in their lives and marriage.

When a marriage reflects God's eternal design, it becomes a powerful testimony to the world — a living parable of Christ's love for His Church, of spiritual authority in unity, of covenant love that speaks life, of family life as discipleship in action, and of a marriage

A Love Worth Waiting: Hapily Ever After

in constant growth. May these truths inspire you to embrace a marriage that glorifies God in every aspect.

1. Marriage Is a Reflection of Christ and the Church

In a kingdom marriage, the union mirrors the divine relationship between Christ and His Church. As Ephesians 5:25 instructs,

"Husbands, love your wives, even as Christ also loved the church, and gave himself for it."

In this sacred pattern:

- The husband leads with humility and sacrificial love, echoing Christ's selflessness.

- The wife honors her husband with grace and strength, reflecting the Church's respectful submission and adoration.

- Together, both partners forgive, serve, and endure—with every act, their marriage proclaims His message without uttering a word.

Imagine a couple whose everyday actions—be it a quiet word of encouragement or an act of service—speak volumes without pretense. Their life together becomes a living sermon, where the tender care in times of trouble and the mutual sacrifice in daily living point unmistakably to Christ's redemptive love. As Ellen G. White wrote, the true home is one where "Christ's character is imprinted on every member, transforming the relationship into a lasting beacon of divine fellowship" (The Adventist Home).

2. Godly Marriage Multiplies Spiritual Authority

When two believers unite under God's guidance, their combined faith produces a spiritual authority that magnifies the power of their prayers. Matthew 18:19 promises: "Again I say unto you, That if two of you shall agree on earth as touching any thing, it shall be done for them of my Father which is in heaven."

In practice, a husband and wife praying together create an environment where faith is strengthened and miracles are set in motion. When challenges arise — or when the weight of the world seems heavy — they stand united in prayer, witnessing the transformative power of God's Word in action. Their joint petitions become a testament to spiritual unity and a mighty force against the adversities of life. This unity blesses their home and impacts their community, demonstrating that the combined might of two believers can move mountains.

3. Covenant Love Preaches to a Broken World

A kingdom marriage is more than a private affair — it is an open witness. When a couple routinely forgives each other, chooses one another daily, and prioritizes Christ above all, every gesture becomes a proclamation of the

A Love Worth Waiting: Hapily Ever After

Gospel. John 13:35 declares: "By this shall all men know that ye are my disciples, if ye have love one to another."

Consider the impact of a couple who, even in the midst of trials, demonstrates unwavering compassion and mercy. Their willingness to extend grace in difficult moments and commit anew to each other each day serves as a luminous example of God's unconditional love. By placing their covenant above personal interests, they radiate hope and trust in Christ—a powerful message to a world that desperately needs the light of the Gospel.

4. Raising a Family Becomes Discipleship in Action

Children in a kingdom marriage are not a mere pause in ministry; they are an active extension of it. The exhortation in Deuteronomy 6:6–7 reminds parents to diligently teach their children:

"And these words, which I command thee this day, shall be in thine heart... and thou shalt teach them diligently unto thy children."

In a home where biblical values are lived out daily, every meal shared, every prayer whispered, and every bedtime story becomes an opportunity for discipleship. The family unit transforms into the first church—a mission field where God's wisdom and love are sown into the hearts of the next generation. When a couple models prayer, service, and unwavering faith, they create an environment where children grow in spiritual maturity, learning to embrace the commandments of God as naturally as they learn to walk and talk. As Ellen G. White noted, the family is "the first classroom of heaven," where God's teachings take root and flourish (The Adventist Home).

5. A Marriage on Mission Is Constantly Growing

A kingdom marriage is not a static destination, but an ongoing journey marked by continual growth and transformation. Proverbs 4:18 wisely observes:

"The path of the just is as the shining light, that shineth more and more unto the perfect day."

In such a marriage, both partners learn to:

- Communicate with honor, ensuring every conversation reflects respect and truth.

- Forgive quickly, letting go of grievances before they fester.

- Serve joyfully, finding delight in each opportunity to honor God and each other.

- Hear God together, listening intently to His guidance as they navigate life's complexities.

A Love Worth Waiting: Hapily Ever After

- Say "yes" to assignments—even when inconvenient—as part of their mutual mission to serve.

This dynamic process of growth and renewal means that a kingdom marriage continuously evolves—becoming brighter, deeper, and more attuned to the call of God. Even in imperfection, the journey of pursuing God together refines their character and magnifies their testimony.

The truth of a kingdom marriage unfolds in every facet of the union. It is a reflection of Christ's love, a multiplier of spiritual authority, a public proclamation of the Gospel, an active discipleship in family life, and a journey of constant growth. When a couple embraces these truths, their marriage becomes not only a source of personal joy but also a living ministry that points others to the transformative power of God's love.

May these reflections encourage you to build and nurture a marriage that is authentically Kingdom-oriented—a union that steadfastly reflects the heart of Christ and becomes a radiant testimony of His love in a broken world.

A Love Worth Waiting: Hapily Ever After

Did You Know?

According to the *Barna Group*, couples who pray together regularly are **92% more likely** to stay married long-term and are **significantly more involved in church and mission work**.

A shared spiritual life isn't just nice — it's **essential** for marital strength and eternal fruitfulness.

Prayer for a Marriage on Mission

Lord, let our love be more than emotional — let it be eternal. Use our marriage as a vessel of hope, healing, and testimony. Teach us to serve one another, and together serve You. Let our covenant glorify You in public and in private. Let our children rise up and call us blessed. Let our home be heaven's outpost. Amen.

A Love Worth Waiting: Hapily Ever After

Reflection Questions

1. What is the mission of our marriage — beyond loving each other?

2. How can we better reflect Christ in how we speak, forgive, and serve?

3. Are we praying together consistently — and inviting God into our decisions?

4. How is our home impacting others for eternity?

Journal Prompt

Write out a "Marriage Mission Statement." What do you want your marriage to be known for? How do you want to serve others together? What legacy are you building for your future children and community?

A Love Worth Waiting: Hapily Ever After

Chapter 15
The First Year: How to Build Without Breaking

"Through wisdom is an house builded; and by understanding it is established." – Proverbs 24:3

After the Vows, Real Life Begins

The dress is packed away. The honeymoon fades into memory. The gifts are opened. And now... it's just the two of you.

What no one tells you is that the first year of marriage is both beautiful and brutally honest.

You begin to see **the real person** — not just the dating version. Old routines meet new expectations. Two wills, two histories, two personalities must learn to dance — without stepping on each other.

The first year doesn't define the whole marriage. But it lays a foundation. **A cracked beginning can be repaired — but a strong one blesses for decades.**

"The work of transformation must begin with the union of hearts and lives... this is a training time." — Ellen G. White, The Adventist Home, p. 100

A Love Worth Waiting: Hapily Ever After

Story: When Perfect Met Pressure

Daniel and Rebeca had been best friends before marrying. Everyone thought they were perfect. But six months in, Daniel shut down emotionally, and Rebeca felt rejected.

They weren't fighting — but they weren't thriving either.

Instead of hiding the cracks, they humbly reached out for help. Through pastoral mentoring, weekly prayer together, and a lot of forgiveness, they slowly rebuilt not just passion — but **partnership**.

Their testimony today? "We thought we were strong. But the first year made us seek the Lord like never before — and that's what made us unbreakable."

What to Expect in the First Year (And How to Build Right)

These insights offer a realistic look into the transitional stage of early marriage—where differences emerge, communication is refined, expectations are realigned, old habits are reshaped, and forgiveness is learned daily. Grounded in Scripture, these truths invite you to build a marriage that is both resilient and Christ-centered.

A Love Worth Waiting: Hapily Ever After

1. You'll Discover Differences You Didn't See Before

In the quiet unfolding of married life, you'll notice new facets about one another—how your partner organizes their space, cleans up, manages finances, and processes emotions. These differences, once unnoticed, now play a significant role in your daily life. As Philippians 2:3 reminds us, "Let nothing be done through strife or vainglory; but in lowliness of mind let each esteem other better than themselves."

Rather than allowing these differences to become battlegrounds for conflict, celebrate them. Recognize that each unique trait contributes to the richness of your shared life. Create systems that honor both your strengths and quirks instead of engaging in power struggles. For instance, if one of you is meticulous about tidiness while the other is more relaxed, try to agree on household roles and routines that respect both preferences. This mindset—rooted in humility and mutual respect—lays the foundation for lasting unity.

2. Your Communication Style Will Be Tested

Communication is the lifeblood of any relationship, and in the first year, various styles—be it silence, sarcasm, evasiveness, or even aggressive remarks—may surface. To build right, any negative habits must be consciously unlearned. Proverbs 15:1 teaches us, "A soft answer turneth away wrath: but grievous words stir up anger."

The solution is to develop the art of active, non-defensive listening and to speak truth with grace. Practice using "I feel" statements to share your inner thoughts without casting blame—for example, "I feel hurt when…" rather than "You always…" This approach not only defuses tension but also brings clarity and warmth to your conversations, paving the way for deep and meaningful connection.

3. Sexual Expectations May Not Match Reality

In our media-driven culture, sexuality is often portrayed as flawless and spontaneous. However, reality involves learning curves, emotional nuance, and the development of true intimacy over time. As 1 Corinthians 7:3 instructs, "Let the husband render unto the wife due benevolence: and likewise also the wife unto the husband."

Your first year together is a period of discovery, where sexual expectations must be discussed openly rather than assumed. Approach these differences with patience, transparency, and a willingness to seek godly guidance if needed. Remember that sexual intimacy is not a performance to be perfected overnight—it's a sacred covenant expression that deepens as emotional connection and trust are built gradually.

A Love Worth Waiting: Hapily Ever After

4. Old Habits May Clash with New Covenant

Before marriage, you each developed personal habits in areas such as money management, scheduling, devotional practices, and stress response. After uniting in a new covenant, these habits may clash as you begin to live "as one." As 2 Corinthians 5:17 declares, "If any man be in Christ, he is a new creature…"

This is an invitation for both of you to create shared rhythms that honor your new identity together. Consider establishing joint routines for budgeting, daily or weekly prayer, planning for the future, and even setting aside intentional sabbath times for rest and renewal. By building a "new us," you affirm that your marriage is a dynamic partnership where old patterns are reformed to reflect the grace and unity found in Christ.

5. You'll Need to Re-Learn Forgiveness — Daily

In close, everyday living, it is inevitable that moments of hurt or frustration will occur. Two imperfect people will sometimes fail one another. Colossians 3:13 reminds us, "Forbearing one another, and forgiving one another… even as Christ forgave you, so also do ye."

The key is to prevent small offenses from piling up. Embrace a lifestyle of swift apology and free, unconditional forgiveness. Keep short accounts and make forgiveness a daily practice—a habit that clears your heart of bitterness and rebuilds trust continuously. In doing so, you create a resilient bond that mirrors the grace and restorative power of the Gospel.

The first year of marriage is a period of profound growth and adjustment—a time when differences become opportunities for deeper understanding and communication evolves into a tool for unity. As you navigate sexual realities, reconfigure old habits, and re-learn forgiveness daily, you are invited to build your marriage on the unshakable foundation of God's Word. By celebrating differences and overcoming challenges with grace, you set the stage for a lifelong journey marked by love, humility, and mutual transformation.

May this comprehensive guide inspire you as you build right in your first year of marriage, trusting that every step—every challenge and every victory—is part of God's divine design for a loving, transformative union.

Did You Know?

Research from the Gottman Institute shows that the first year of marriage is critical for **habit-setting**. Couples who develop regular **check-ins**, **shared prayer**, and **emotional attunement** in their first 12 months are **dramatically more likely** to stay together long-term and report higher satisfaction.

A Love Worth Waiting: Hapily Ever After

The habits you build now will either bless or burden the decades ahead.

5 First-Year Foundations to Build Together

The first year of marriage is a critical period during which you establish core habits, create shared values, and build an unshakable foundation that reflects both your commitment to one another and to God. Grounding every aspect of your relationship in intentional practices not only helps you navigate initial challenges but also sets the stage for a lifetime of mutual growth, support, and spiritual depth. As Ecclesiastes 4:9–10 proclaims, "Two are better than one: for if they fall, the one will lift up his fellow."

Embrace these five foundational areas to build your first year—and your future—on solid, kingdom principles.

1. A Weekly Sabbath for Your Relationship

Set aside a regular night each week as a dedicated Sabbath—a time free of the distractions of phones, work, and worldly concerns. This intentional pause is designed for just the two of you to focus on one another and to connect with God. Whether it's a candlelit dinner, a quiet walk under the stars, or simply unplugging and sharing your hearts over a home-cooked meal, this weekly Sabbath becomes a sacred ritual. As you commit to this practice, you'll notice that the intentional downtime deepens your intimacy and invites God's presence to renew your energy and perspective week after week. Consistent, undistracted time together cultivates a resilient bond and paves the way for spiritual growth in your union.

2. A Conflict Resolution Plan

Disagreements are a natural part of any intimate relationship. In your first year together, it is vital to create a clear conflict resolution plan that outlines how you will talk, listen, and de-escalate disagreements when they arise. Remember the wisdom of Proverbs 15:1: "A soft answer turneth away wrath: but grievous words stir up anger."

Agree in advance to use gentle, honest language and to avoid tactics such as silence, sarcasm, or personal attacks. Develop strategies like taking a brief time-out if emotions run high, using "I feel" statements to express your perspective, or even scheduling regular check-ins to discuss any underlying issues before they ignite into larger conflicts. This proactive approach not only minimizes hurt feelings but also strengthens the foundation of trust and respect that is essential for a thriving marriage.

A Love Worth Waiting: Hapily Ever After

3. A Financial Vision

Money matters are among the most significant practical considerations in early marriage. Establishing a shared financial vision—complete with agreed-upon budgets, savings plans, and goals for giving—creates a unified path forward. Work together to map out your financial priorities: discuss how you handle money, set clear targets, and plan how to celebrate both small wins and larger milestones. A transparent financial plan isn't just about balancing a checkbook; it's about building a life in which both partners are on the same page regarding stewardship of God's resources. When you align your financial practices, you foster an atmosphere of trust and cooperation that permeates every aspect of your partnership.

4. A Spiritual Altar

Designate regular time as your couple's spiritual altar—a dedicated space for prayer, Bible study, and shared dreams. This might be a set time each morning or a weekly evening session where you both come together to delve into Scripture, pray for your future, and set spiritual goals. Establishing this ritual provides a constant reminder that your marriage is not only about complementing each other, but also about growing together in godliness. This practice nurtures your heart, aligns your individual will with God's purpose, and invites divine guidance into your decision-making. As you reflect on His Word side by side, you forge a spiritual connection that will sustain your marriage through every season of life.

5. A Support Circle

No marriage is an island. Building a supportive network is crucial for your ongoing health as a couple. Cultivate a support circle of trusted mentors, seasoned married couples, and close friends whose wisdom and perspectives can guide you through challenges and celebrate your successes. This support system provides accountability and serves as a resource for encouragement and prayer during tough times. As Ecclesiastes 4:9-10 reminds us, the strength of two — and even more — is far superior to facing the journey alone. Lean on these godly voices to gain fresh insights, receive constructive feedback, and be reminded that your union is part of a larger, community-centered-plan.

The first year of marriage is a time of discovering, adapting, and building on shared dreams. Establishing a weekly Sabbath dedicated to your relationship, formulating a conflict resolution plan, creating a unified financial vision, dedicating time to your spiritual altar, and surrounding yourselves with a support circle are foundational steps to ensure your union is both resilient and reflective of God's love. By embracing these practices, you lay the groundwork for

A Love Worth Waiting: Hapily Ever After

a marriage that is not only strong in the present but also built to endure all of life's seasons.

May these five foundational steps empower you to build a first year—and a lifetime—of mutual love, growth, and Christ-centered partnership, ensuring that your marriage strengthens and uplifts you both in every way.

Prayer for the First Year

Lord, thank You for the gift of covenant. Teach us to walk slowly, to love deeply, and to build wisely. Let this first year be our garden of trust — where roots grow, walls fall, and Your Spirit reigns. Make us strong in our weakness. United in our difference. And joyful in the journey. Amen.

A Love Worth Waiting: Hapily Ever After

Reflection Questions

1. What old habits am I bringing into marriage that I need to surrender?

2. How do I tend to react when conflict arises — and how can I grow?

3. What kind of culture do I want in my home (tone, rhythms, language)?

4. Who are the mentors we can turn to when storms come?

Journal Prompt

Write a "first year vision prayer." Describe the emotional, spiritual, and relational atmosphere you hope to create together. What will be your non-negotiables? What legacy begins now?

Chapter 16
Crisis-Proofing Your Covenant: How to Stand When the Storm Hits

"And the rain descended, and the floods came, and the winds blew, and beat upon that house; and it fell not: for it was founded upon a rock." – Matthew 7:25, KJV

Storms Are Not Optional — Collapse Is

Every marriage will face a crisis.

It may come as a financial blow, a miscarriage, an emotional disconnect, the death of a loved one, job loss, infertility, infidelity, or depression.

Storms test your **foundation** — not your love songs.

But when your marriage is anchored in Christ, every storm becomes an opportunity:

- To fight *together*, not *against* each other
- To grow deeper instead of breaking apart
- To emerge stronger, wiser, and more united

"God tests the endurance and faith of those whom He blesses. He strengthens their character and reveals His power in their weakness." — Ellen G. White, The Ministry of Healing, p. 471

Story: Their Marriage Nearly Sank — Until God Rebuilt It

Carlos and Julia had been married for seven years when Julia found messages from another woman on his phone. The pain was unbearable. Trust shattered.

Carlos wept in repentance. Julia considered leaving. But through counseling, fasting, and a lot of pastoral mentoring, they slowly rebuilt trust.

"It was the darkest season of my life," Julia said. "But also the most sacred. Because I met Jesus in the ruins of my marriage — and He raised it from the dead."

7 Crises That Can Shake a Marriage

These challenges are not mere hypotheticals — they are real storms that can test the strength and resilience of a marital relationship. Yet, with preparation, reliance on God's grace, and a commitment to walk together through every trial, you can face these crises head-on and emerge stronger as a couple.

1. Infidelity (Emotional or Physical)

Infidelity strikes at the very heart of trust and intimacy. Whether it manifests emotionally or physically, the betrayal can shatter the foundation of a marriage, leaving deep wounds and lingering doubts. In times of such pain, turn to God's healing promise. Psalm 51:10 pleads, "Create in me a clean heart, O God; and renew a right spirit within me."

The journey toward restoration requires sincere repentance, transparent communication, and often the guidance of trusted mentors or professional counseling. While the scars may remain, God's grace can foster forgiveness and, if both partners are willing, a path to rebuilding trust.

2. Financial Hardship or Job Loss

Financial stress—whether through hardship or unexpected job loss—can quickly become a significant burden on a marriage. The strain of diminished resources, mounting bills, and uncertainties about the future may lead to frustration and conflict. Yet, Scripture offers comfort and assurance. Philippians 4:19 declares, "But my God shall supply all your need according to his riches in glory in Christ Jesus."

In such seasons, couples can come together to create a realistic financial plan. Open discussions about budgeting, sacrifices, and long-term goals can transform financial crisis into an opportunity for unified growth and trust in God's provision.

3. Death of a Child or Close Family Member

The loss of a child or a beloved family member is one of the most excruciating experiences any couple can endure. This grief can create a profound void and may lead to emotional distance if not navigated with care. Yet, God is near to the brokenhearted. Psalm 34:18 comforts us with the promise, "The LORD is nigh unto them that are of a broken heart; and saveth such as be of a contrite spirit."

In this deep sorrow, turning to each other, seeking solace in prayer, and engaging with a supportive community can help mend broken hearts. While grief may never entirely vanish, shared faith and mutual support pave the way for gradual healing.

4. Mental Health Issues (Anxiety, Depression)

Mental health challenges like anxiety and depression can cast long shadows over a marriage. When one or both partners struggle with internal battles, feelings of isolation and misunderstanding may arise. Scripture encourages us to lean on God in times of turmoil. Philippians 4:6-7 advises,

"Be careful for nothing; but in every thing by prayer and supplication with thanksgiving let your requests be made known unto God. And the peace of God, which passeth all understanding, shall keep your hearts and minds through Christ Jesus."

A Love Worth Waiting: Hapily Ever After

Reaching out for professional help, practicing empathy, and maintaining open communication can help bridge the gap. By turning to prayer and each other, couples can find a renewed sense of hope and mental well-being.

5. Addiction or Substance Abuse

Addiction—whether to substances, behaviors, or other forms of dependency—poses a serious threat to the sanctity of marriage. It breaks trust and often spirals into cycles of destructive behavior. Yet, the transformative power of Christ offers a way out. 1 Corinthians 10:13 assures, "There hath no temptation taken you but such as is common to man: but God is faithful, who will not suffer you to be tempted above that ye are able."

Confronting addiction often requires professional intervention, genuine repentance, and a steadfast commitment to recovery from both partners. With the support of a loving community and reliance on God's strength, healing and restoration are possible.

6. Spiritual Coldness or Backsliding

A marriage marked by spiritual decline—where prayer, worship, and mutual encouragement diminish—can leave partners feeling emotionally adrift. Spiritual coldness can invite feelings of isolation and disillusionment. Revelation 2:4 gently warns, "Nevertheless I have somewhat against thee, because thou hast left thy first love."

Reigniting spiritual intimacy is vital. Recommit to regular times of shared worship, Bible study, and prayer. This renewed focus on God's presence can refresh your hearts and rekindle the passion that first drew you together.

7. Prolonged Emotional Disconnect or Apathy

Over time, the daily routines and challenges of married life may lead to a prolonged emotional disconnect or apathy. The initial spark may seem to fade as both partners become consumed by the pressures of life. Colossians 3:13 encourages,

"Forbearing one another, and forgiving one another, if any man have a quarrel against any: even as Christ forgave you, so also do ye."

Addressing emotional disconnect requires intentional efforts—regular, heartfelt conversations, shared activities, counseling, and a renewed commitment to each other. Overcoming apathy is an ongoing process of listening, understanding, and consistently seeking to deepen your connection.

These seven crises—infidelity, financial hardship, loss, mental health struggles, addiction, spiritual coldness, and emotional disconnect—are formidable storms that can shake a marriage to its core. Yet, you need not be paralyzed by fear. With preparation, unwavering faith, prayerful communication, and reliance on God's promises, you and your spouse can weather these challenges together. Remember that every challenge presents an opportunity to lean more fully on God and each other, turning trials into testimonies of His grace and the strength of your unity.

May this reflection empower you to prepare for life's storms with wisdom, courage, and the abiding presence of God, trusting that every trial faced together can ultimately draw you closer to Him—and to each other.

How to Crisis-Proof Your Covenant

1. Build Your Marriage on the Rock (Not Feelings)

"Except the Lord build the house, they labour in vain that build it…" – Psalm 127:1, KJV

Love must be deeper than romance. It must be rooted in *Christ's covenant*, not culture's feelings.

Crisis will expose your foundation. Build wisely now.

A Love Worth Waiting: Hapily Ever After

2. Establish a Prayer Life Before Trouble Comes

When the waves hit, you won't learn to swim — you'll cling to what you already know.

"Call unto me, and I will answer thee…" – Jeremiah 33:3, KJV

Make prayer a reflex, not a last resort.

3. Invest in a Safe, Supportive Community

No couple should ever weather a crisis alone. You need people who will:

- Pray without judgment
- Speak life
- Offer wise counsel
- Stand in the gap when your strength runs out

"Bear ye one another's burdens, and so fulfil the law of Christ." – Galatians 6:2, KJV

4. Practice Emotional Honesty, Not Suppression

Stuffed pain turns into bitterness. Unspoken hurt becomes disconnection.

Learn to say:

A Love Worth Waiting: Hapily Ever After

- "I'm afraid."
- "I feel alone."
- "I don't know what to do — let's pray."

Vulnerability is the bridge to restoration.

5. Learn to Fight *for* Each Other — Not *with* Each Other

"Be ye angry, and sin not: let not the sun go down upon your wrath." – Ephesians 4:26, KJV

In every storm, you have a choice:

- Fight the wind, or each other
- Focus on fault, or join in faith
- Curse the darkness, or seek the Light

Did You Know?

According to a longitudinal study by the National Marriage Project, couples who actively engaged in **faith-based practices** (like shared prayer and community support) were **over 50% more likely to recover from crisis** than those who attempted to resolve problems alone.

A Love Worth Waiting: Hapily Ever After

Faith is not just comfort — it's *crisis armor*.

3 Covenantal Promises for the Storm

1. "I will not run — I will stay and fight with you."
2. "I will seek God's solution — not my comfort."
3. "I will believe our story is not over — because God is still writing."

Prayer for the Storm

Lord, the winds are rising. But so is our faith. We will not give up. We will not let the enemy take what You've joined. Teach us to hold each other tighter when the world shakes. Be the center of our covenant. Restore what is broken. Anchor us, Jesus. Amen.

A Love Worth Waiting: Hapily Ever After

Reflection Questions

1. What personal or shared crises have shaken our faith in each other?

2. Do we have a plan for staying emotionally and spiritually connected in hardship?

3. Who is our spiritual support system when we feel weak?

4. What foundation are we really building on?

Journal Prompt

Describe a storm you've walked through — as a couple or alone. What did it reveal about your character, your faith, and your emotional patterns? What would you do differently today with Christ at the center?

A Love Worth Waiting: Hapily Ever After

Chapter 17
When Love Is Hard: Grace for Marriages in Survival Mode

"My grace is sufficient for thee: for my strength is made perfect in weakness." – 2 Corinthians 12:9, KJV

When "I Do" Feels Like "I Can't"

Some days, love feels effortless. Other days, it feels like a war zone. And sometimes — it doesn't feel like anything at all.

There are moments in every marriage when the **feelings fade**, the spark dims, and you're left staring across the table at someone you hardly recognize… or someone who no longer sees you.

And in those moments, you ask:

- Is love supposed to feel this lonely?
- Did I marry the wrong person?
- Is it too late to fix this?

A Love Worth Waiting: Hapily Ever After

This chapter isn't for the fairytale stage — it's for the *faith battle*. And if that's where you are, here's what you need to know:

You are not alone. You are not a failure. And your story is not over.

"Satan is constantly at work to weaken the marriage union, and to bring it into disrepute. It is the work of God's people to strengthen and elevate it." — Ellen G. White, The Adventist Home, p. 346

Story: What They Almost Gave Up

Natalie and Isaac were both active in ministry. But behind closed doors, they lived separate lives. Years of miscommunication, small offenses, and growing distance left their love dry.

They considered separation. But one day, a counselor said something simple: *"Before you walk away, give God space to work."*

It wasn't instant. But over time — through honesty, hard conversations, prayer, and therapy — they started rebuilding. Brick by broken brick.

Today they say: "We didn't find our way back to each other — we found our way back to Jesus. And He led us home."

A Love Worth Waiting: Hapily Ever After

Signs Your Marriage May Be in Survival Mode

These signs are not merely surface-level concerns; they reveal deep patterns of disconnection and distress that indicate a marriage is barely hanging on. Recognizing these warning signals is the first step toward seeking help, healing, and restoration — reminding you that God is near even in the midst of trials.

1. Avoidance of Meaningful Conversation

When couples steer clear of deep, vulnerable dialogue, they miss the opportunity to connect, understand, and heal together. This avoidance can leave unresolved issues festering in the background, slowly eroding emotional intimacy. Without honest conversation, potential misunderstandings grow and become barriers between you. True connection requires open hearts and minds, where both partners feel safe to share their hopes, fears, and disappointments. As in every healthy relationship, intentional communication is the glue that binds hearts even when life gets complicated.

2. Physical Intimacy That Is Absent or Forced

Physical intimacy is a natural expression of love and closeness. When it becomes absent or, conversely, feels coerced and mechanical, it signals that the natural rhythm of affection has been disrupted. A marriage built solely on routine or obligation rather than mutual desire can lead to feelings of rejection and loneliness. In a thriving partnership, physical closeness should reflect the emotional and spiritual bond shared between two people. Without this, the physical aspect of your relationship may lose its life-giving power and become another area of contention.

3. Feeling More Like Roommates Than Partners

When daily interactions feel akin to simply sharing a space rather than building a life together, it's a clear sign that something vital is missing. Instead of experiencing the warmth of a loving team, you find yourself coexisting in parallel lives with little genuine connection. This sense of detachment turns your marriage into a series of functional tasks rather than a shared journey of growth, joy, and support. Without intentional effort to celebrate each other and nurture your partnership, it's all too easy to slide into a state of mere cohabitation.

4. Escalated or Unresolved Small Arguments

In a healthy marriage, disagreements are opportunities to learn and grow. However, when minor conflicts spiral into major disputes or, equally harmful, are left unaddressed, it creates a cycle of tension and bitterness. Repeated, unresolved arguments can chip away at respect and trust, making every interaction a potential battleground. The destructive pattern here is not about the conflict itself, but the lack of healthy conflict resolution skills—which leave wounds that never fully heal.

5. Unspoken Resentment and Silent Sadness

When frustration, hurt, or disappointment is never voiced, it tends to settle into unspoken resentment. Over time, these silences can build a heavy atmosphere of sadness and isolation. Instead of feeling understood and loved, you may begin to question whether your partner really cares at all. Unspoken expectations and unmet needs eventually transform into a quiet sorrow that shadows your daily life—diminishing the joy that your union was meant to bring.

6. Secret Considerations of Divorce

Perhaps the most alarming sign is when divorce—even if only contemplated privately—enters your thoughts. When you find yourself weighing separation as an option, it's a stark indicator that the marriage is in survival mode. The very idea of divorce, while complex and often painful, reflects a deep-seated yearning for escape from ongoing distress. It is a signal that the foundation of the relationship has been compromised to such a degree that the pain can seem unbearable.

A Love Worth Waiting: Hapily Ever After

A Call to Hold On

If these signs resonate, take heart. God is not only present in thriving marriages but is especially near to those that feel crushed and barely holding on. Scripture comforts us in Psalm 34:18 (KJV):

"The LORD is nigh unto them that are of a broken heart; and saveth such as be of a contrite spirit."

Your current struggles are not the final chapter. With honest reflection, prayerful communication, and often professional guidance or counseling, there is hope. God's love is transformative—even in the darkest moments—and He longingly invites you into restoration, renewal, and deeper intimacy.

A marriage in survival mode is marked by the avoidance of meaningful conversation, a loss, or distortion of physical intimacy, a shift toward sharing space like roommates, recurrent unresolved conflicts, underlying unspoken resentment, and even thoughts of divorce. These warning signs, while painful to acknowledge, also call for urgent, compassionate intervention. Whether through counseling, renewed prayer, or rebuilding communication channels, remember that you are not alone. God's grace is abundant for every bruised relationship, and His presence is especially real for those who are hurting.

May this reflection empower you to recognize the signs and to seek the help necessary to move from mere survival toward a thriving, restored marriage—

knowing that God stands close, ready to bring healing to every broken heart.

What to Do When Love Feels Hard

When the well of love seems to run dry or when emotional distance casts a shadow over your relationship, these five steps can help restore the connection. Rooted in Scriptural truths, they invite you to lean not on your effort but on divine intervention, open honest dialogue, trusted counsel, persistent forgiveness, and prayerful intercession.

1. Return to the Source of Love — Jesus

When love feels hard, it isn't because you need extra human effort—it's that you need divine intervention. In times when your feelings run dry or when the spark seems to have dimmed, return to Jesus, the inexhaustible source of love. As 1 John 4:10 beautifully reminds us: "Herein is love, not that we loved God, but that he loved us…"

This verse tells us that the love which transforms lives flows from God's initiative. When you feel that your love is faltering or growing weak, take the time to pray, study His Word, and let the Holy Spirit refresh your heart. His love is constant, and when you allow it to fill you anew, you gain the strength to love your spouse even more deeply.

2. Speak Truth — with Humility

Honesty and vulnerability are key to reopening the channels of connection. Rather than masking your pain or hiding behind a facade, share your struggles with humility — not to cast blame but to be truly known by your partner. As Ephesians 4:15 exhorts: "Speak the truth in love…"

Choose a quiet moment where both of you can engage without distraction. Use "I feel" statements to express your emotions thoughtfully and avoid accusations. Learning to speak your truth with grace creates a safe space where genuine healing and understanding can flourish. This process clears away pretenses and invites a renewed sense of intimacy built on mutual respect and honesty.

3. Bring in Safe Help

Healing is not meant to be done in isolation. When love feels hard, sometimes the burdens are too heavy to bear alone. Trusted pastors, Christian counselors, mentors, or wise friends can be part of God's rescue team in your marriage. Proverbs 11:14 teaches: "Where no counsel is, the people fall: but in the multitude of counsellors there is safety."

When silence has allowed hurt and misunderstandings to take firm root, invite safe help. Seeking counsel is not a sign of weakness but of wisdom — it opens the door to new perspectives, healing, and consistent support. Remember, by sharing your struggles with others, you dismantle the strongholds that come with isolation.

4. Forgive — Again and Again

Bitterness is a slow poison that can distort every experience in your life if left unaddressed. Holding on to the past hurts and creates a lens through which every action is viewed with suspicion or pain. Ephesians 4:32 encourages us: "And be ye kind one to another, tenderhearted, forgiving one another, even as God for Christ's sake hath forgiven you."

Forgiveness is not about excusing the offense—it's about releasing its power over you. It is a daily, intentional act of letting go. When you practice forgiveness, you clear away the residue of bitterness, paving the way for true healing and a deeper, more resilient love. Embrace forgiveness as a repeated, liberating act that continuously transforms your heart and your marriage.

5. Fast and Intercede

Some battles in love have deep, spiritual roots that require more than just human effort. Fasting and prayer are powerful disciplines that invite divine intervention into emotional struggles. In Matthew

A Love Worth Waiting: Hapily Ever After

17:21, we are reminded that: "This kind goeth not out but by prayer and fasting."

When you face spiritual or emotional drought, commit to a season of fasting and intercession—both individually and together. When your spouse is unable to pray or is emotionally shut down, stand in the gap for them. Ask God for breakthroughs, for the softening of hardened hearts, and for miracles that only He can provide. This disciplined reliance on Him shifts the power of the battle from your own finite strength to the infinite power of the Creator.

When love feels hard, do not resign yourself to inevitable disconnection. Instead, return to the Source of Love—Jesus—who never runs dry. Speak truth with humility to reopen the door to intimacy, bring in safe help to bolster your efforts, continuously practice forgiveness to break the chains of bitterness, and resort to fasting and prayer to combat the deeper spiritual roots of emotional struggle. By embracing these steps, you invite the transformative power of God into your relationship, guiding you toward healing and renewed love.

May these reflections empower you to rekindle love even when it feels hard, trusting that the divine power of God is always ready to restore and renew the bonds of your marriage.

A Love Worth Waiting: Hapily Ever After

Did You Know?

Couples in crisis who commit to at least 12 weeks of counseling, coupled with individual spiritual growth, have **up to a 70% success rate** in rebuilding trust and reconnecting emotionally — even after infidelity or long-term disconnect. Source: American Association of Christian Counselors (2022)

What Grace Looks Like in Marriage

This reflection illustrates that grace is not simply a set of actions but a heart posture—a continual outflow of divine love that transforms how we relate to one another. When grace fills our marriage, it transcends our natural tendencies, enabling us to act in ways that reflect the kind of love described in Scripture.

1. Grace Listens When You'd Rather Walk Away

Grace is evident when, in moments of tension or hurt, you choose to pause and listen instead of fleeing the conversation. It is that deliberate choice to give your spouse the benefit of your full attention, even when frustration tempts you to turn away. In doing so, you open the door for understanding and healing. Rather than letting silence become a barrier, grace allows you to hear not only the words being spoken but also the underlying pain, hopes, and desires. This act of listening creates space for reconciliation and fosters a secure environment where vulnerability becomes a strength.

2. Grace Says "I'm Sorry" Even When You Feel Justified

Occasionally our pride and sense of righteousness can make it hard to apologize. Yet, grace empowers us to humble ourselves and offer a sincere "I'm sorry." When you choose forgiveness over self-justification, you clear away the obstacles that block true intimacy. Saying "I'm sorry" is not an admission of weakness but an act of courage; it signals that your commitment to love transcends the need to be right. It is a reminder that in marriage, healing takes precedence over winning an argument. This willingness to humble yourself reflects the heart of God's grace—a grace that covers every shortcoming and restores broken bonds.

3. Grace Seeks to Understand Before Demanding to Be Understood

True grace moves us to pause and seek understanding, rather than immediately demanding that our perspective be acknowledged. Before you insist on being heard, ask your spouse to share their feelings and thoughts completely. This approach defuses conflict and cultivates a deeper connection built on mutual respect. By choosing to understand first, you demonstrate that the relationship—and the person you love—are more important than proving a point. In that posture of listening, you mirror the compassionate heart of Christ and create a foundation where both partners feel secure in expressing themselves.

4. Grace Gives Time, Space, and Prayer — But Doesn't Give Up

Marriage is a journey that sometimes demands patience beyond our immediate capacity. Grace is evident when you give your partner the time and space they need to process emotions, all while maintaining a steadfast commitment to the relationship. Offering time and space is not about withdrawing; rather, it is about allowing healing to occur naturally without pressure. In those moments of quiet reflection and prayer, you invite God's transformative power to work on both your hearts, reminding you that the struggle is not permanent and that there is hope for renewed intimacy. Grace perseveres—it remains present even when circumstances seem bleak, underscoring the truth that love endures.

5. Grace Remembers: This Is a Covenant, Not a Contract

One of the deepest expressions of grace in marriage is the understanding that your union is a covenant—a sacred promise that goes far beyond a mere legal agreement or temporary arrangement. A covenant is marked by unconditional commitment and lifelong grace. It is not contingent on flawless performance but on the enduring promise to love, honor, and support one another in every season. Reminding yourself that marriage is a covenant helps shift the focus from transactional exchanges to an everlasting bond. It

A Love Worth Waiting: Hapily Ever After

enables you to see every challenge not as a breach of contract, but as an opportunity to grow together in faith and love. This perspective empowers you to extend kindness and patience, even when the road is rough.

A Foundation in Divine Love

The biblical passage of 1 Corinthians 13:4-7 encapsulates what grace in marriage looks like: "Love suffereth long, and is kind; love envieth not; love vaunteth not itself, is not puffed up Doth not behave itself unseemly, seeketh not her own, is not easily provoked, thinketh no evil; Rejoiceth not in iniquity, but rejoiceth in the truth; Beareth all things, believeth all things, hopeth all things, endureth all things."

Each line of this passage offers a blueprint for grace — emphasizing that true love endures hardships, celebrates truth, and ultimately casts out fear. In your marriage, embodying these qualities is a testimony not only to each other but also to the living Word of God.

What grace looks like in marriage is both simple and profound: it is listening when you feel like walking away, apologizing when pride says otherwise, seeking to understand rather than instantly being understood, giving time and space while persisting in love, and always remembering that your union is a sacred covenant rather than a casual contract. When you choose to live out these principles, you invite the

A Love Worth Waiting: Hapily Ever After

transforming power of God's love into your marriage, turning even the ordinary moments of life into extraordinary expressions of divine grace.

May this reflection inspire you to embrace and exemplify grace within your marriage, fostering an environment where love, understanding, patience, and divine commitment transform every interaction into a reflection of God's perfect design.

Prayer for Marriages in Survival Mode

Jesus, we're tired. We're hurting. We've forgotten how to be soft, how to feel close. But we don't want to give up. Come into our covenant. Bring life to what feels dead. Give us the strength to stay, to forgive, to hope, and to fight. We put this marriage back in Your hands. Amen.

A Love Worth Waiting: Hapily Ever After

Reflection Questions

1. What parts of my marriage have gone numb — and why?

2. Am I praying for my spouse more than I'm criticizing them?

3. Have we invited anyone safe into our process of healing?

4. Do I believe God can still redeem and restore this covenant?

Journal Prompt

Write a raw, honest letter to God about your current state of marriage (or your fears about it). Don't censor your pain. Then write His response back to you — words of hope, truth, and a future you want to believe again.

Chapter 18
When You're Married to Someone Who Doesn't Share Your Faith

"For what knowest thou, O wife, whether thou shalt save thy husband? or how knowest thou, O man, whether thou shalt save thy wife?" – 1 Corinthians 7:16, KJV

Loving with Unequal Light

You wake up early to pray. You go to church alone. You read Scripture, tears in your eyes, wondering if your spouse will ever meet the Savior who changed your life.

You love them. But you ache. You speak of hope. They respond with silence. You grow deeper in Christ… and feel farther from them.

This is what it means to live in an **unequally yoked marriage**.

Maybe you married before you knew Christ. Maybe they drifted away. Maybe you disobeyed God and chose a relationship He never blessed.

Wherever you are now — God sees your pain, and He hasn't given up on your home.

A Love Worth Waiting: Hapily Ever After

"The Lord is very pitiful, and of tender mercy." – James 5:11, KJV

Story: She Prayed for 25 Years

Beatriz married Luis when they were both secular. She met Jesus at a women's conference and was baptized soon after.

Luis called it a "phase." But it wasn't. It was her new identity. She served, gave, and worshiped — and he stayed home.

For 25 years.

But one night, broken by life and softened by time, Luis asked, "Can we pray?"

He was baptized six months later. Today, they teach baptismal classes together.

Beatriz says, "God didn't just save Luis. He saved my heart from despair."

What It Means to Be Unequally Yoked

This meditation delves into the spiritual and practical realities of forming intimate partnerships—with a focus on marital relationships—when the foundational beliefs and values differ. It invites you to consider not

A Love Worth Waiting: Hapily Ever After

only the challenges but also the extraordinary level of grace, patience, and supernatural love required to hold such a union together.

Understanding the Yoke

In biblical terms, a yoke was used to bind two oxen together so that they could plow a field in unison. The command in 2 Corinthians 6:14 admonishes, **"Be ye not unequally yoked together with unbelievers…"**

This scripture cautions that when two are joined together, but do not share the same spiritual heritage, the plow—symbolic of the shared mission and direction of life—runs the risk of veering off course. When one partner is stronger, weaker, or simply has a different set of values, the weight of conflicting beliefs can pull the couple away from a unified purpose.

The Spiritual Reality of Unequally Yoked Marriages

When applied to marriage, being unequally yoked often means that while the hearts remain tied together, they pull in different directions. Couples may experience a persistent tug-of-war over priorities, with one partner focused on building a relationship grounded in Christ-like values and the other perhaps prioritizing worldly pursuits. The disparity may surface in decisions about finances, parenting, or spiritual growth, and over time, these differences can lead to tension, miscommunication, and even division.

Although the biblical directive focuses on sharing the same spiritual foundation, it does not imply that God is incapable of working in a union where disparities exist. However, such relationships demand double the grace, double the patience, and a supernatural kind of love that only comes from a deep reliance on the Holy Spirit. In these unions, every decision, every moment of conflict, and every act of love can become an arena for demonstrating the transformative power of God's grace.

The Call for Extraordinary Grace

The challenges inherent in an unequally yoked marriage call for extraordinary measures. It is not enough for each partner to rely solely on personal willpower; a continual, divine intervention is necessary. This means engaging deeply in prayer, seeking spiritual counseling, and cultivating a commitment to grow together despite differences. By asking the Lord to guide your steps, you invite His unifying power to mend weaknesses and align your hearts.

It is precisely in these difficult dynamics that the beauty of grace can shine. When differences seem insurmountable, the couple must lean into prayer and

A Love Worth Waiting: Hapily Ever After

mutual compromise—endeavoring to lift each other up even when the natural pull seems to expose the gaps. This kind of love does not wait for perfection; it works actively through imperfections, relying on the promise that in Him, all things are possible.

Living with the Yoke: A Balancing Act

Imagine two oxen at the start of a plowing season. When both are yoked equally, they move harmoniously toward their goal. If, however, one is less willing or comes from a very different pace, the plow may suddenly take an unexpected turn. In the context of marriage, if one partner's faith or values diverge significantly from the other's, the shared journey can quickly become unstable. The partnership may require recalibrating priorities, investing more in spiritual discussions, or even setting aside regular times for joint worship and reflection to re-align your direction.

Developing strategies for harmony in the face of such disparity might include engaging in Bible studies together, discussing what it means to live out your faith daily, and committing to mutual goals that transcend personal differences. The more intentional both partners are about cultivating a shared direction, the more likely they are to find unity even in the midst of differing tendencies.

A Love Worth Waiting: Hapily Ever After

What It Means to Be Unequally Yoked is not just a warning but also an invitation. It challenges couples to evaluate whether they are walking together in step toward a common, God-centered purpose. While an unequally yoked marriage presents significant hurdles, these obstacles can be overcome by relying on double the grace, double the patience, and a supernatural kind of love. By prioritizing spiritual unity and seeking divine guidance, couples can strive to move in harmony—even when the yoke itself is imbalanced.

May this reflection encourage you to seek a relationship where your hearts pull in the same direction—a union gracefully married to the truth of God's word, sustained by His power, and enriched by His love.

How to Love Someone Who Doesn't Share Your Faith

This reflection invites you to embrace the challenge of loving unconditionally while still holding firm to your own spiritual convictions. It's not about forcing change with words or pressure; it's about letting your life be a living testimony to the love and transformation you have received from God.

1. Live the Gospel — Don't Just Preach It

True transformation is witnessed in the way you live. As 1 Peter 3:1 instructs wives to be in subjection so that even without words, the gospel may win hearts, the same principle applies when loving a partner who doesn't share your faith.

"**Likewise, ye wives, be in subjection... that, if any obey not the word, they also may without the word be won by the conversation of the wives.**" - 1 Peter 3:1

Nagging, criticism, or overt pressure will not win a soul over. Instead, let your peace, joy, patience, and purity shine forth in your everyday life. By embodying the gospel values through actions and character, you allow the transformative power of Jesus to speak louder than words ever could. Your life becomes the ultimate witness—a gentle but profound invitation toward the love that changes everything.

2. Pray Like Their Salvation Depends on It — Because It Might

Prayer is one of the most effective ways to support your spouse spiritually. James 5:16 reminds us that the fervent prayers of a righteous person are powerful: "**The effectual fervent prayer of a righteous man availeth much.**" - James 5:16

Commit to praying consistently:

- **For Their Heart to Be Softened:** Ask the Lord to gently work in your spouse's heart, opening their eyes to His love.

- **For God to Bring People into Their Life:** Invite friends, mentors, or fellow believers who might encourage them on a spiritual journey.

- **For Moments of Conviction and Clarity:** Pray for flashlights to shine into the hidden corners of their soul.

- **For Guidance on When to Speak and When to Remain Silent:** Seek the discernment of the Holy Spirit; sometimes silence is the greatest loving act, while other moments call for gentle counsel.

Such intercessory prayer not only supports your spouse—even if you don't see immediate change—but also strengthens you, anchoring your hope in God's timing and wisdom.

3. Stay Spiritually Anchored

Loving someone who shares a different faith perspective can be challenging if you allow your own spiritual life to drift. As 1 Corinthians 16:13 exhorts: "Watch ye, stand fast in the faith, quit you like men, be strong."

It's vital to remain firmly anchored in your spiritual disciplines. Fast, worship, and stay engaged in a supportive community so that you—and, by extension, your relationship—do not fall prey to compromise. Guarding your soul by nurturing your relationship with God will not only sustain your personal well-being but will also model a vibrant faith that might one day inspire your partner to explore deeper spiritual truths.

4. Set Grace-Filled Boundaries

Loving someone who doesn't share your core beliefs requires both respect for their space and a commitment to protecting your spiritual rhythms. Romans 12:18 advises: "If it be possible, as much as lieth in you, live peaceably with all men."

Boundaries are essential—not to isolate, but to ensure that within your home and relationship, Christ is honored. These boundaries might include dedicated times for personal prayer, clear limits on topics that stir conflict, or designated family times when unfettered worship and discussion of faith occur. By creating an environment where your convictions are respected and visible, you establish a peaceful home that reflects Christ's character, giving your partner a glimpse of the transformative power of a life lived for God.

5. Don't Lose Hope — But Let God Set the Timeline

Remember that salvation is a process, not an instant transformation. Galatians 6:9 (KJV) encourages perseverance: "Be not weary in well doing: for in due season we shall reap, if we faint not."

A Love Worth Waiting: Hapily Ever After

Hold on to hope even when progress seems slow. Trust that God is more invested in your spouse's soul than you are, and that He knows the perfect time for their heart to be softened. While you continue to love unconditionally, let God set the timeline. Keep your focus on being a faithful witness and support system, and remember that your role is to love—and to pray—while God works in ways that might surpass your expectations.

Loving someone who doesn't share your faith is a journey marked by grace, humility, and unwavering commitment. It begins by living the gospel through your everyday actions rather than mere speech, advancing through fervent prayer, staying anchored in your spiritual life, creating grace-filled boundaries, and ultimately, holding on to hope as God orchestrates His divine timing. Through these practices, you become a living testament to God's love—a beacon of hope that may, in time, illuminate the path toward spiritual reconciliation.

May this reflection guide you as you navigate the complex journey of loving someone who doesn't share your faith, trusting that your unwavering dedication and the power of God's love can work miracles even in the most challenging circumstances.

A Love Worth Waiting: Hapily Ever After

Did You Know?

A study from the Pew Research Center found that **15% of marriages begin unequally yoked**, but among those who stay faithful and spiritually consistent, **over 35%** of unbelieving spouses eventually come to faith.

The number one factor? Persistent love without pressure.

What About the Children?

This meditation addresses the challenges of raising children in a home where one spouse may not actively support spiritual training, yet reminds you of the authority and responsibility you have in Christ to nurture your children in His ways.

The Biblical Mandate for Spiritual Training

The command in Deuteronomy 6:7 states: "And thou shalt teach them diligently unto thy children…"

This is not merely a recommendation—it is a divine mandate. Despite any differences in household perspectives on spiritual education, God entrusts you with His truth. Your role as a parent is to ensure that your children are exposed to and taught the foundational principles of love, grace, and truth. Even if your spouse does not actively champion spiritual training, you still have authority and responsibility in Christ to shape your children's hearts. The Bible makes clear that a child's spiritual formation begins at home, through both instruction and example.

When you commit to this task, you are building a legacy that will affect not only your family but also future generations. The work you do in guiding your children is a reflection of God's own character—persistent, loving, and truth-filled. Remember that this calling is both a privilege and a serious responsibility, as it requires intentionality, perseverance, and continual reliance on God's grace.

Practical Ways to Nurture Spiritual Growth

1. Bring Them to Sabbath School. Regular attendance at Sabbath school or Christian educational programs provides your children with a community of believers and a consistent environment for learning biblical truths. In this setting, they witness how faith is lived out and are exposed to God's Word in a structured and nurturing atmosphere. By integrating Sabbath school attendance as a natural part of your family's routine, you create opportunities for your children to ask questions, grow in understanding, and experience the love of a faithful community. Even if your spouse is less enthusiastic about these gatherings, your commitment to making them a priority can establish a strong spiritual foundation for your kids.

2. Pray with Them. Prayer is the lifeblood of a vibrant spiritual life. When you pray with your children, you model an intimate relationship with God and demonstrate that spiritual communication is not reserved for moments of crisis—it is a daily expression of trust and love. Set aside time as a family to pray together. Whether it's a simple prayer at bedtime, before meals, or during quiet moments in the morning, these practices remind your children that they are never alone. They learn that God is always near and that their lives are deeply interwoven with His care, regardless of differing opinions in other areas of the home.

3. Teach Them Love, Grace, and Truth. Beyond structured activities, everyday moments present opportunities to impart the values of love, grace, and truth. Demonstrate forgiveness, patience, and kindness in both word and deed, showing your children what it means to extend unconditional love and live according to biblical principles.

Engage your children in discussions about Scripture, share stories of God's faithfulness, and explain how these principles should shape their decisions and interactions. By consistently reinforcing these values, you provide them with a moral compass that will guide them through the complexities of life—even if the spiritual climate in the home is not uniformly supportive.

Even in a family where one spouse may not fully support spiritual training, the authority, and responsibility in Christ remain yours. "What About the Children?" becomes not an excuse to compromise on imparting truth, but a call to action—to lead by example, invest in meaningful spiritual practices, and persist in teaching your children the love, grace, and truth of God. Remember, the transformation of a child's heart is a gradual process shaped by consistent, diligent teaching. As you fulfill this calling with prayer, intentional teaching, and by relying on God's strength, you set up your children for a lifetime of spiritual growth and a legacy of faith.

May this reflection inspire you to be bold in your efforts to nurture your children's faith, trusting that God will honor your diligence as you fulfill His eternal mandate.

Prayer for the Unequally Yoked

Lord, I feel torn. I love this person, but I ache for them to know You. Give me patience to live the gospel when words don't work. Give me strength to stand in faith. Help me not to lose joy. I entrust their salvation to You. Open their eyes, awaken their heart, and prepare our home for redemption. Amen.

A Love Worth Waiting: Hapily Ever After

Reflection Questions

1. Am I modeling the love of Christ in my home?

2. Have I surrendered my spouse to God — or tried to control their journey?

3. How can I stay spiritually filled without my partner's support?

4. What victories can I celebrate, no matter how small?

📝 Journal Prompt

Write a letter to your unbelieving spouse — one you may never give them. Pour out your hope, pain, and desire for them to know God. Then write a letter from God to you — full of His comfort, promise, and strength.

A Love Worth Waiting: Hapily Ever After

Chapter 19
God in the Mundane: Finding Heaven in Dishes, Laundry, and Bills

"And whatsoever ye do, do it heartily, as to the Lord, and not unto men." - Colossians 3:23, KJV

More Laundry Than Love Songs

Marriage isn't made up of grand gestures every day. It's made of grocery lists, morning breath, tired smiles, and dishes that never seem to end.

Romance often fades into routine. But what if the **routine is where God shows up the most?**

What if folding laundry, paying bills, cleaning up messes, and driving to appointments could become acts of **worship**?

"It is not the great things we do, but the little things, faithfully done, that reveal the character of Christ in the home." — Ellen G. White, The Adventist Home, p. 254

The sacred doesn't only live in the sanctuary — it dwells in the sink.

A Love Worth Waiting: Hapily Ever After

Story: A Love Lived in Quiet Ways

Every Friday night, José cleaned the kitchen while Ruth lit candles and set out the Sabbath meal. They'd been married 42 years. He didn't write poetry. She wasn't great with words.

But every time he brought her a clean glass without being asked, or folded her favorite blanket, she saw love.

"We've had hard years," Ruth said. "But he never stopped showing up in the small things. That's how I know his love is real."

Where Heaven Meets the Everyday

This reflection invites you to see how simple, daily tasks can become sacred acts of love and service when done with a heart focused on God. Every ordinary chore is an opportunity to reflect Christ's character and nurture your marriage, transforming routine responsibility into an outpouring of divine grace.

1. Dishes = Servanthood

As Jesus taught in Matthew 23:11: **"But he that is greatest among you shall be your servant."**

When you wash a plate or tackle the dishes, you're not simply cleaning up a mess. You are practicing a form of servanthood—a tangible expression of humility and care. In the everyday act of doing the dishes, you honor your spouse by showing that love is lived out in the small details and that no task is beneath you. It becomes an act that speaks volumes about your commitment to serve, even when no one is watching.

Reflect: How can I serve today without being asked or applauded? Consider asking yourself how you might quietly take initiative in the home, demonstrating that true greatness in marriage is measured by the willingness to serve.

2. Laundry = Covering in Grace

Think of the everyday cycle of laundry—washing, folding, and putting away clothes. It is a task that rarely garners praise, but it embodies love's subtle, yet essential, presence. Much like love, which is often invisible yet profoundly felt, taking care of the laundry is an act of grace that blankets your home with warmth and care.

Reflect: How can I meet a need before it becomes a complaint? By noticing small unspoken needs within your household—perhaps a favorite shirt needing mending or a pile of laundry forgotten—you have the chance to cover your loved ones in grace and thoughtfulness before a minor oversight grows into frustration.

3. Paying Bills = Provision and Partnership

Budgets may not be the most romantic aspect of marriage, but they speak to a deeper commitment. Romans 12:17 encourages us: "Provide things honest in the sight of all men."

Managing finances well is a form of stewardship. When you approach paying bills with honesty, planning, and cooperation, you're not only securing your family's needs, but you're actively partnering in the work of building something eternal. By handling your household resources with care, you protect the temple of your marriage and create a space where love and trust can thrive.

Reflect: Are we building something eternal with our resources? Ask yourselves if your financial practices are aligned with your long-term spiritual and relational goals—ensuring that every dollar and decision honors your shared commitment to God's provision.

4. Cooking = Nourishment and Creativity

Cooking is much more than preparing a meal; it is an act of nourishing both body and soul. As you prepare food, you are crafting an environment where connection can flourish. The imagery of Jesus revealing Himself at a dinner table (Luke 24:30–31) reminds us that even ordinary meals can become extraordinary moments of encounter and grace.

A Love Worth Waiting: Hapily Ever After

Reflect: Is our table a place of stress or of joy, warmth, and gratitude? Take time to consider whether your mealtimes are infused with conversation, prayer, and a spirit of celebration, or if they've devolved into mere routines. Cultivate a table where every dish served becomes an invitation to connect and rejoice together.

5. Routine Rhythms = Worship in Motion

Love in marriage often resembles the steady, rhythmic beat of a heart rather than sporadic, overwhelming bursts of passion. Routine acts—those small, repeated gestures of care—are the foundation upon which a lasting love is built. Luke 16:10 tells us: "He that is faithful in that which is least is faithful also in much…"

Every predictable, everyday task performed with love and faithfulness becomes a form of worship in motion—an ongoing, living sacrifice that shapes your soul. Whether it's waking up at the same time each day to share a cup of coffee or maintaining a silent prayer together in the quiet moments before bed, these routines reflect a commitment that transcends the ordinary.

Reflect: Am I faithful in the unnoticed places? Ask yourself how you can be faithful and intentional in the small tasks—those unnoticed moments that, cumulatively, define the character and strength of your marriage.

A Love Worth Waiting: Hapily Ever After

When everyday tasks are viewed through the lens of faith and service, they become much more than chores—they become avenues for expressing heavenly love on earth. Whether it's serving through washing dishes, covering your family with grace through laundry, stewarding your resources as a faithful partner, nourishing each other through cooking, or establishing routine rhythms of worship in the small moments, each act is a chance to embody Christ's selfless love.

May this reflection inspire you to see your daily routines as opportunities to honor God and your spouse, turning ordinary tasks into extraordinary acts of love that transform your home into a place where heaven meets the everyday.

May these reflections help you embrace the sacred in the mundane, discovering that every aspect of your daily life is an opportunity to worship, serve, and express the love of Christ in your marriage.

Did You Know?

A study from the University of Virginia's National Marriage Project found that couples who express appreciation for **small daily tasks** (like making coffee, washing dishes, or packing lunch) report **higher levels of overall happiness and emotional connection** than couples who focus only on "quality time."

A Love Worth Waiting: Hapily Ever After

Gratitude in the mundane makes love sustainable.

How to Invite God into the Everyday

In the ordinary moments of life, God's presence can transform routine tasks into acts of worship and reflection. When you intentionally invite God into the details, every task becomes a sacred opportunity to draw near to Him, deepen your spiritual life, and cultivate an atmosphere of love and grace in your home.

1. Pray While You Clean

Imagine turning something as mundane as washing dishes into a spiritual encounter. Instead of simply scrubbing away grime, view your sink as an altar — an opportunity to converse with God in the quiet moments of routine. As you clean, let your thoughts be filled with prayer, gratitude, and petitions, transforming a daily chore into a sacred dialogue with the Creator. This intentional act cleanses the physical space and refreshes your spiritual heart, reminding you that even the simplest task can be a holy act.

Reflect: How can I invite God into even this moment of cleaning, letting His presence transform routine chores into times of worship?

A Love Worth Waiting: Hapily Ever After

2. Speak Blessings Over Your Spouse While They Sleep

The bedroom, often a place of rest and refuge, can be transformed into a sanctuary of blessing. Before your spouse wakes, speak words of love, encouragement, and prayer over them. Blessing your spouse as they sleep is an intimate act that softens hearts and builds a gentle atmosphere of care. It's a quiet, profound way of inviting God's peace into your home, setting a tone of spiritual intimacy that transcends the night and prepares the heart for a new day.

Reflect: What simple, loving words can I speak that will uplift my spouse, inviting God's grace into our personal retreat?

3. Celebrate the Ordinary

Everyday moments are filled with small acts that often go unnoticed—but they are opportunities to celebrate God's goodness. Whether it's saying thank you for the little acts of kindness, smiling when folding clothes, or lighting a candle at dinner, these simple gestures become avenues for worship. In celebrating the ordinary, you remind yourself and your family that God is present even in the smallest details. Such awareness transforms a normal day into a series of sacred moments, each one a reminder of His constant love and care.

A Love Worth Waiting: Hapily Ever After

Reflect: How can I intentionally celebrate these small blessings and invite gratitude into every moment of my day?

4. Create Sacred Rhythms

Consistency in the everyday can anchor your spiritual life. Set aside even five minutes of shared Scripture reading or Sabbath preparation to form sacred rhythms within your home. These regular, intentional habits become the beat that steadies your week—quiet times that develop consistency in faith, foster mutual anticipation for God's guidance, and weave a consistent thread of His presence throughout your daily lives. Over time, these moments collectively create a sanctuary in your home where every rhythm points back to God.

Reflect: Are there small moments in my day that I can dedicate to inviting God to be part of our rhythm—a daily appointment that sets the tone for the rest of our week?

Inviting God into the everyday isn't about grand gestures or elaborate rituals. It's about transforming ordinary tasks into sacred acts—turning a sink into an altar with prayerful cleaning, blessing your spouse while they sleep, celebrating the small joys, and creating recurring moments of spiritual connection. When you adopt these practices, you begin to see every moment as an opportunity to encounter the divine. In doing so, you create a home where God's light shines through daily, and where every task, no matter how simple, becomes a testament to His enduring presence.

May this reflection inspire you to embrace the sacred in the mundane, inviting God into every aspect of your daily life so that His presence continually transforms the ordinary into something extraordinary.

Prayer for the Mundane

Lord, I want to see You in the small things. Teach me to love through acts that go unseen. Make me faithful in the daily, tender in the practical, joyful in the quiet moments. Let my home become a holy place — not because of perfection, but because You live here. Amen.

Reflection Questions

1. Have I missed God's presence in the ordinary routines of marriage?

2. Do I serve with joy — or with quiet resentment?

3. What small act could become sacred if done with love and intention?

4. How can we create rhythms that welcome God into our daily life?

A Love Worth Waiting: Hapily Ever After

📝 Journal Prompt

List five small ways your spouse serves you regularly — and thank God for each. Then list five new ways you want to serve your spouse more intentionally this week.

A Love Worth Waiting: Hapily Ever After

A Love Worth Waiting: Hapily Ever After

Chapter 20
The Prayer-Filled Home: Building an Atmosphere Where the Spirit Dwells

"And let them make me a sanctuary; that I may dwell among them." – Exodus 25:8, KJV

More Than a House — A Dwelling Place for God

- You can have a beautiful house…
- A clean floor…
- A cozy bed…
- But if prayer is absent — **peace will be too.**

Prayer isn't just something couples should do — it's what **transforms your home into a sanctuary**. It invites God into your schedule, your kitchen, your bedroom, your future, and your children's hearts.

"Those who seek God in the home will be blessed. Angels will minister to them. A holy atmosphere will pervade their home." — Ellen G. White, The Adventist Home, p. 31

A Love Worth Waiting: Hapily Ever After

A prayer-filled home doesn't mean a perfect home. It means a home where God is invited **into the imperfections.**

Story: Prayer Saved Their Marriage

Ana and Martín were on the brink. Constant fighting. Emotional coldness. Even talking about separation.

Then one night, a friend texted: "Fast and pray for 7 days. Don't fix your marriage — invite God into it."

So they did. They fasted. They anointed their door. They sat together and said just five words: *"Jesus, please live here again."*

Everything didn't change at once. But something broke in the Spirit. Healing began. Kindness returned. And slowly, **God didn't just fix the marriage — He reigned in the home.**

Why Prayer Changes the Atmosphere

In our daily routines lie hidden opportunities to encounter the divine. By intentionally transforming ordinary tasks into acts of worship, you create a life where God's presence permeates even the simplest moments. This approach not only enriches your spiritual life but also brings profound peace and unity into your home.

A Love Worth Waiting: Hapily Ever After

1. Pray While You Clean

Turn your sink and countertop into an altar. Rather than viewing cleaning as a mundane chore, allow it to become a sacred time of communion with God. As you wash dishes or dust the shelves, invite the Spirit into every sweep and scrub. Imagine that each plate, each utensil, is being refreshed not only physically but spiritually — a reminder that God can make every task an act of worship.

Reflect: Can I transform my routine cleaning into a joyful, prayerful encounter with God?

2. Speak Blessings Over Your Spouse While They Sleep

The quiet before dawn offers a unique, intimate moment to bless your spouse. As they rest, whisper words of encouragement, love, and prayer. Let your bedroom become a sanctuary where peace reigns and God's favor is spoken over every soul that sleeps there. These gentle blessings not only nurture your partner's spirit but also set a tone of tenderness and grace in your home.

Reflect: What loving words can I share quietly that will envelop my spouse with a sense of God's care?

3. Celebrate the Ordinary

Everyday moments often hide extraordinary blessings. Smile when folding clothes, thank your family for the small acts of kindness they show, and light a candle at dinner to remind each other of the light of Christ even in darkness. These simple acts are expressions of gratitude that acknowledge God's goodness in every detail of life. By celebrating the ordinary, you begin to see that life itself is a continuous reason to give thanks.

Reflect: How can I intentionally pause to give thanks for the small blessings in our day?

4. Create Sacred Rhythms

Consistency in our daily routines forms the backbone of a vibrant spiritual life. Even setting aside five minutes of shared Scripture reading or Sabbath preparation can anchor your week and deepen your connection with God. Establish these regular moments of prayer, meditation, or worship as non-negotiable appointments with the Divine. Over time, these sacred rhythms become the pulse of your home, infusing every aspect of your life with intentional holiness.

Reflect: What daily sacred moments can I create that will make our home a continual place of spiritual renewal?

A Love Worth Waiting: Hapily Ever After

Inviting God into the everyday means recognizing that even the simplest tasks—cleaning, speaking kind words, celebrating small acts, and establishing daily rhythms—can be transformed into opportunities for encountering His presence. By consciously embracing these practices, you shift from viewing routine chores as burdens to seeing them as moments of grace and worship. In doing so, you create an atmosphere where heaven truly meets the everyday, and every action becomes an offering to the One who transforms all things into sacred moments.

May these reflections inspire you to see every moment as an opportunity to invite God's presence, transforming the ordinary into a series of divine appointments that nurture your soul and bless your home.

Did You Know?

Studies from Harvard University's Human Flourishing Project show that families who pray together regularly are significantly more likely to experience:

- Lower stress and anxiety
- Higher levels of gratitude
- Greater emotional regulation
- Deeper interpersonal connection

Even science agrees: prayer isn't just powerful — it's **transformational.**

5 Habits of a Prayer-Filled Home

These habits transform everyday moments into sacred encounters with God, nurturing spiritual intimacy in your family and home. Each practice invites God's presence and builds a foundation of unity, peace, and love that can sustain your household through all of life's seasons.

1. Start the Day in Prayer Together

Begin each morning by gathering as a family — even if it's just for 2-3 minutes. Hold hands, speak words of blessing over the day, and invite the Holy Spirit to guide every step. This simple, shared moment sets a positive tone and fosters a sense of togetherness that can ripple through all your daily interactions.

Reflect: Consider how a few minutes of intentional prayer can shift your mindset for the entire day. Can you create a morning routine that blends gratitude, hope, and purpose into your start?

2. Create a Prayer Space or Altar

Dedicate a small area in your home to prayer. It might be a quiet corner adorned with a Bible, candles, a favorite chair, or meaningful prayer cards. By making this space visually sacred, you remind yourself and your family that God is always near — even in the hustle of everyday life.

Reflect: How might a dedicated prayer corner help you and your family refocus during stressful moments or transitions? What items would make the space meaningful and inviting?

3. Bless Meals with Intention

Transform mealtime into an opportunity to declare more than just gratitude. Instead of simply saying grace, take a moment to speak blessings over your food — declare peace, health, provision, and thanks. This practice turns an ordinary meal into a powerful reminder of God's continuous care and sustenance.

Reflect: In what ways can you move beyond a routine prayer at the table? How might intentional blessings over your food nurture a more profound awareness of God's provision in your daily life?

4. End the Day in Prayer

Before bed, cover each other in prayer. As you close your day, speak words of encouragement and gratitude over every family member — mention your children by

A Love Worth Waiting: Hapily Ever After

name, ask for rest and restoration, and invite God's protection to carry you all into peaceful sleep. This practice not only calms the spirit but also builds trust in God's constant presence even in the quiet hours of the night.

Reflect: What small rituals might help you transition from the busyness of the day to a state of reflective peace? How can you personalize your bedtime prayers to honor each family member's needs?

5. Pray When There's Conflict

When tensions rise, pause the argument and choose prayer as your first response. Take a moment to hold hands, breathe deeply, and say aloud, "Let's ask God to help us hear each other." This intentional pause can defuse anger, soften stubborn hearts, and open up the space for honest dialogue. By inviting God into the conflict, you transform a potentially divisive moment into a turning point for healing and reconnection.

Reflect: How can you cultivate the habit of pausing to pray amid disagreement? Consider the impact of synchronous, heartfelt prayer in turning conflict into a catalyst for deeper understanding and unity.

A prayer-filled home is not built overnight; it is nurtured by small yet powerful habits that invite God into every corner of your life. Starting and ending the day in prayer, creating a dedicated space for God,

A Love Worth Waiting: Hapily Ever After

blessing meals with intention, and turning moments of conflict into opportunities for divine intervention lay the groundwork for a household where heaven and everyday life seamlessly merge. As these habits take root, you'll find that every aspect of your family life becomes a living testimony to faith, gratitude, and the transformative power of God's love.

May these reflections inspire you to weave prayer into the fabric of your everyday routines, transforming your home into a sanctuary of God's love, peace, and enduring presence.

Prayer for a Prayer-Filled Home

Holy Spirit, we don't want just a peaceful house — we want a dwelling where You abide. Teach us to pray with passion, patience, and purpose. Make our home a place where angels dwell, children grow in faith, and strangers feel heaven. Let this house be filled with Your glory. Amen.

A Love Worth Waiting: Hapily Ever After

Reflection Questions

1. Is prayer a habit in our home — or a reaction to crisis?

2. What spiritual atmosphere do I feel in our living space?

3. How do I model a life of prayer to my spouse or children?

4. What is stopping us from praying together more often?

📝 Journal Prompt

Design a "Prayer Rhythm" for your home. What time will you start the day in prayer? What place will you dedicate as sacred? Who will you pray for? What promises will you speak over your family daily?

Chapter 21
Leaving a Legacy: Love That Echoes into Eternity

"A good man leaveth an inheritance to his children's children…" – Proverbs 13:22, KJV

When Love Outlives You

One day, the voices in your home will quiet. The dishes will stop clinking. The bed will stay made. And the love you lived — in words, in prayers, in service — will be the only thing left echoing in the hearts of those you touched.

Marriage is not just about now. It is about legacy.

Your covenant has the power to shape generations:

- How your children love
- How they forgive
- How they believe
- How they pray
- How they trust God in seasons of loss or joy

You are writing a story. And long after you're gone — your story will still speak.

A Love Worth Waiting: Hapily Ever After

"Thou shalt teach them diligently unto thy children... and shalt talk of them when thou sittest in thine house."
– Deuteronomy 6:7

Story: A Table of Generations

Ruth and Hernando were married 56 years. Every Friday, they gathered their children and grandchildren for a meal. No matter how busy life became, the Sabbath started with worship at their table.

When they passed away, their granddaughter Ana said:

"What I remember most isn't the food. It was the way Grandpa touched Grandma's hand while praying. It was the way they forgave each other quickly. Their love taught us who God is."

Today, Ana and her husband lead a young family ministry. The echo continues.

The Power of a Godly Legacy

In your daily life together, each act—whether big or small—becomes a testimony of God's love and grace. When you live out your marriage with integrity, it serves as an ever-present sermon to those around you. Explore below how your commitment can influence your household and generations to come:

A Love Worth Waiting: Hapily Ever After

1. Your Marriage Becomes a Living Sermon

As 2 Corinthians 3:2 declares, "Ye are our epistle, written in our hearts, known and read of all men."

While you might not stand on a pulpit to preach, your marriage itself is a written testimony to the outside world. Every kind word, every act of service, and every moment of mutual sacrifice speaks of the Gospel in action. Your faithfulness and commitment become a living sermon—a visible, powerful witness that invites others to see Christ through your relationship. In living out your covenant commitment, you not only honor God but also inspire those who observe the grace and love within your home.

Reflect: How can my daily actions at home become a testament to God's love—visible to friends, family, and even strangers?

2. Your Children Learn How to Love by Watching You

Proverbs 20:7 reminds us, "The just man walketh in his integrity: his children are blessed after him."

Your home is the first and most influential classroom your children will ever enter. They absorb what they see—your tenderness in moments of conflict, the humility of your apologies, the healing power of your honesty, and the transformative effect of your prayers. Every kind gesture and every moment of integrity becomes part of their blueprint for love. By living out a marriage marked by genuine care and spiritual depth, you provide your children with a legacy of love that shapes their future relationships.

Reflect: What everyday expressions of love are my children witnessing, and how are these shaping their understanding of true, God-centered love?

3. Your Consistency Makes Room for Generational Blessing

Luke 1:50 proclaims, "His mercy is on them that fear him from generation to generation."

Every consistent, God-honoring choice you make in your marriage is an investment in the future—not only for you and your spouse, but for the generations that follow. When you commit to living faithfully in the small details, you sow seeds that may yield blessings far beyond your lifetime. Your daily consistency in following God's principles builds a firm foundation, ensuring that the legacy of love and obedience will be passed on to your children, grandchildren, and great-grandchildren.

Reflect: How can my commitment to small, daily acts of obedience and grace unlock blessings that extend into future generations?

A Love Worth Waiting: Hapily Ever After

4. Your Marriage Can Heal the Past

Isaiah 58:12 offers hope for breaking negative cycles: "And they shall be called, The repairer of the breach…"

Often, cycles of divorce, addiction, anger, or fear have marred family legacies. Yet, by living out a marriage that reflects God's redemptive love, you have the power to break those chains. Your steadfast commitment and willingness to forgive can turn a history of pain into a story of healing and new beginnings. In being "the repairer of the breach," your marriage becomes a bridge to a future where the scars of the past are replaced by the hopeful promises of God's grace.

Reflect: In what ways can our marriage become a healing force—one that transforms past hurts into the hope of a brighter, redeemed future?

Your marriage is not just a private relationship—it is a living, breathing sermon. Whether through your daily acts of love, the example you set for your children, the consistent choices that lead to generational blessings, or the healing power you hold to break destructive cycles, your life together speaks volumes. Embrace this truth: your marriage, grounded in God's wisdom and love, is a powerful testimony that can transform hearts and shape futures.

May these reflections inspire you to view your marriage as a ministry—a living sermon that not only transforms your own lives but also blesses those who are blessed to witness it.

Did You Know?

A study from the University of Notre Dame found that children who observe consistent **spiritual devotion and parental love** in the home are:

- 70% more likely to remain in the faith
- More resilient during trauma
- More likely to form healthy romantic relationships
- More involved in church and community as adults

Legacy isn't theory. It's impact.

How to Build a Marriage That Echoes Beyond You

When your marriage is not only for your own joy but becomes a legacy that influences future generations, every word, action, and tradition takes on eternal significance. By embracing habits that declare God's faithfulness, model forgiveness, celebrate commitment, and bless your family, you create a marriage whose influence extends far beyond your lifetime.

A Love Worth Waiting: Hapily Ever After

1. Pray Aloud — and Often

In your marriage, let prayer be a vibrant, audible expression of your faith. When you pray aloud, you invite not only God's presence into your daily life but also set a powerful example for your children, family, and guests. Imagine your conversation with God filling the home with a spirit of peace and encouragement — each prayer becomes a declaration of trust in His love and power. This consistent outpouring of faith signals that Christ is at the center of your union.

Reflect: Ask yourself: How can my everyday prayers transform our home into a sanctuary where God's name is spoken with love and confidence?

2. Tell Stories of God's Faithfulness

A marriage that echoes beyond you is steeped in memories of God's miraculous provision and grace. Sharing personal testimonies of how God has shown up in your life — whether at moments of joy or through trials — at the dinner table or during family gatherings not only grounds your marriage in God's truth but also inspires those around you. These stories remind everyone that faith is alive and active in your daily walk.

Reflect: Consider: What memorable moments of God's faithfulness can I recount that will encourage my family and guests to trust Him more deeply?

3. Model Forgiveness That Heals, Not Silence That Shames

Forgiveness is the cornerstone of lasting relationships. When you model forgiveness by offering sincere apologies and seeking reconciliation, you are not only healing wounds in your marriage but also teaching your children how to navigate conflict with grace. Your willingness to say "I'm sorry" and to mend broken bridges becomes a living lesson in humility and love that empowers the next generation to approach mistakes with a healing spirit instead of silence or shame.

Reflect: Ask yourself: How can my own acts of forgiveness create a ripple effect in our family, teaching our children that healing begins with a heartfelt apology?

4. Celebrate Commitment

Commitment is a covenant that deserves celebration. Whether through anniversary traditions, marking faith milestones, or simply acknowledging the small yet significant moments of enduring love, celebrating your commitment infuses your marriage with joy. These celebrations are not just about reminiscing; they are declarations of the promises you've made to each other and to God. By creating joyful traditions, you affirm that your journey is both sacred and worth celebrating, even when the road is long.

Reflect: Consider: What traditions or special celebrations can we introduce that openly honor our ongoing commitment to God and to each other?

5. Write a Blessing Over Your Family

There is power in spoken and written blessings. Committing to write a blessing over your family regularly—whether uttered in prayer, scribed in a journal, or framed on your wall—is a tangible way to proclaim God's grace upon your loved ones. As you repeat this practice year after year, your blessings will become a part of your family history, instilling faith and confidence in each new generation. In doing so, you establish a legacy of hope and divine favor that echoes in the hearts of all who come after you.

Reflect: Ask: How can I incorporate regular, intentional blessings that remind our family of God's promises and enduring love?

Building a marriage that echoes beyond you requires intentionality and daily devotion to practices that honor God and nurture your family. By praying aloud, sharing stories of His faithfulness, modeling healing forgiveness, celebrating your commitment, and writing blessings over your loved ones, you create an enduring legacy of faith. Your marriage then becomes a living sermon — a testimony that inspires others, shapes your children's lives, and extends God's love far into the future.

May these reflections inspire you to build a marriage that not only brings joy and unity in the present but also leaves an indelible imprint on future generations — a legacy of faith, hope, and love that echoes far beyond your own lives.

Prayer to Leave a Godly Legacy

Father, we want more than a good marriage — we want a godly one. One that echoes through generations, one that teaches without words, one that lights a fire in the hearts of our children. Make our home holy. Let our story glorify You, and let our love last long after we are gone. Amen.

Reflection Questions

1. What spiritual legacy was passed down to me — and what do I want to pass on?

2. Are my marriage and home reflecting the love of Christ consistently?

3. What habits or traditions can I start today that will bless future generations?

4. Am I building for convenience — or for eternity?

A Love Worth Waiting: Hapily Ever After

📝 Journal Prompt

Write a letter to your future grandchildren. What do you hope they will say about your marriage? Your faith? Your love? Now write down three decisions you can make today to become that legacy.

A Love Worth Waiting: Hapily Ever After

Chapter 22
Heaven at Home: A Final Charge for Youth in Love

"Thy kingdom come, Thy will be done in earth, as it is in heaven." – Matthew 6:10, KJV

What If Home Could Feel Like Heaven?

What if marriage wasn't just about survival — but about **rehearsing eternity**? What if your kitchen became a place of prayer? What if your bedroom was filled with peace? What if your living room hosted the presence of God?

Heaven is not meant to be a distant destination. It begins **now**, **in you**, and **in your home**.

"Let your light so shine before men, that they may see your good works, and glorify your Father…" – Matthew 5:16

The world is desperate for homes that shine. Children are longing for parents who love without conditions. Hearts are aching for safe places where grace abounds, and Jesus is not a guest — **but the Master of the house.**

Story: A Young Couple Who Became a Living Revival

A Love Worth Waiting: Hapily Ever After

Maya and Caleb were only 26 when they married. They had little money, but much faith. They consecrated their apartment with oil, played worship music while cleaning, read Scripture in the mornings, and prayed before any disagreement.

It wasn't magic — it was intentional. Their home didn't feel big. But it **felt like heaven.** Friends said, *"I feel peace here."* Children said, *"Can we come back tomorrow?"*

And when their first child was born, they whispered, *"Welcome to a holy home, little one."*

What Does Heaven at Home Look Like?

This reflection unveils a vision for a home saturated with God's presence—a place where His love, order, and life-changing grace manifest in every detail. When heaven is at home, every action, every word, and every interaction embodies the divine warmth that transcends human limitations.

1. Jesus Is the Center — Not Just Invited Occasionally

"As for me and my house, we will serve the Lord." - Joshua 24:15

In a home that mirrors heaven, Jesus isn't merely an occasional guest at Sunday services or during a special dinner; He is at the very heart of every moment. He is

A Love Worth Waiting: Hapily Ever After

the Owner who claims your family, the Counselor who guides decisions, and the Friend who walks with you through every joy and trial. His presence should be woven so deeply into your daily lives that the air you breathe speaks of His love and wisdom. A home centered on Christ exudes peace and direction, providing a foundation where every member understands that their identity and purpose are anchored in Him.

Reflect: How might you invite Jesus into each corner of your home—not just at designated times, but as an ever-present partner in your daily routine?

2. Grace Is Spoken More Than Perfection Is Expected

"Mercy rejoiceth against judgment." – James 2:13

In a heaven-at-home, the language of grace is spoken fluently. No one expects perfection in this family; rather, a culture of forgiveness and understanding prevails. You are not raising angels, nor are you in a constant state of flawless union with Christ. Instead, your home is a living testimony of redeemed hearts— where mistakes are met with mercy, apologies are offered freely, and reconciliation is the norm. By valuing grace over unattainable perfection, you create an atmosphere where love overcomes every flaw and healing becomes the common language.

A Love Worth Waiting: Hapily Ever After

Reflect: What steps can you take today to ensure that your home reflects the forgiving and gracious character of heaven even amidst human imperfection?

3. Worship and Prayer Are Daily Atmosphere — Not Rare Events

"Pray without ceasing." – 1 Thessalonians 5:17

A home that echoes with the blessings of heaven is continuously alive with worship and prayer. It's not just about gathering on Sundays; it's in the daily routines—turning mundane chores into moments of devotion, letting background music be replaced by spontaneous praises, and adorning your walls with Scripture that speaks life. When every room resounds with the sound of worship and the soft murmur of prayer, your home becomes a sanctuary where God's presence is palpable, and His peace pervades every conversation and action.

Reflect: How can you transform your daily routines—whether cooking, cleaning, or simply spending time together—into opportunities to worship and connect with God?

A Love Worth Waiting: Hapily Ever After

4. Boundaries Are Clear — But Love Is Unconditional

"He that dwelleth in love dwelleth in God…" – 1 John 4:16

Heaven at home is marked not by chaotic freedom but by lovingly set boundaries that foster security and growth. Clear guidelines and household rules, such as honoring sabbath rhythms and maintaining mutual respect, help preserve an environment of order and beauty. Yet these boundaries are not about control; they are lovingly established to protect the hearts of those within. When the structure of the home is balanced with unconditional love, every rule becomes a testament to God's design—ensuring that while order is maintained, grace flows freely, and relationships are nurtured with kindness.

Reflect: What simple, clear boundaries can you establish or reaffirm in your home that promote safety and growth, all while reflecting unwavering love?

5. The Spirit of Revival Lives in Your Marriage

Revival isn't confined to tent services or singular events—it is a way of life that permeates your daily interactions. Every intentional act that draws you closer to God has the power to ignite a spiritual awakening within your marriage. When you fast and pray, speak blessings over one another, guard your words carefully, choose to love even in difficult times, and

A Love Worth Waiting: Hapily Ever After

remain steadfast when it would be easier to walk away, you transform your union into a living altar. In this dynamic environment, your relationship becomes a beacon of hope and renewal—a continuous revival that strengthens your marriage and radiates God's restorative power to everyone around you.

Reflect: In what practical ways can you nurture a spirit of revival in your marriage so that every day is an opportunity to recommit to God and to each other?

A home where heaven dwells is not built on merely idealized dreams, but on the tangible practices of daily life. When Jesus is placed at the very center, when grace speaks louder than the quest for perfection, when worship and prayer infuse each moment, when loving boundaries are clearly defined, and when a spirit of revival ignites lasting transformation, your home becomes a reflection of heaven on earth. Every act and every word contribute to a legacy that blesses your family and inspires all who encounter your life together.

May these reflections inspire you to create a dwelling where heaven meets the everyday—a home imbued with the grace, order, joy, and revival of God's eternal love.

You become a **living altar.**

A Love Worth Waiting: Hapily Ever After

Did You Know?

Barna Group reports that homes with **daily family prayer**, **weekly intentional worship**, and **shared mission** produce children who are 4x *more likely* to stay in the faith and 2x *more likely* to become spiritual leaders themselves.

Heaven is contagious — especially when it starts at home.

Your Final Commission as Youth in Love

You are not too young.
You are not too late.
You are not too broken.

God is still writing your story. And He's calling you to something radical:

- A love that reflects heaven

- A marriage that builds altars

- A home that births revival

- A legacy that shifts generations

"The kingdom of heaven is like unto leaven..." - Matthew 13:33 Start with your home — and watch the Kingdom rise.

A Love Worth Waiting: Hapily Ever After

Final Prayer

Jesus, let our love be holy. Let our marriage be Yours. Let our home be a gate of heaven. Come dwell in our laughter, our silence, our parenting, our pain. Make our ordinary life extraordinary through Your Spirit. Let the generations after us walk in light — because we chose to love like You. Amen.

Final Reflection Questions

1. What does it mean for heaven to start in my home?

2. What small act of love, prayer, or discipline can shift the spiritual atmosphere today?

3. Who will be impacted eternally by the choices I make in marriage?

4. What is the Holy Spirit asking me to consecrate, surrender, or revive?

Final Journal Prompt

Write a dedication letter. Address it to God. Offer your love, your marriage, your home. Declare that your house will be a place where heaven dwells. Seal it with Scripture and prayer.

A Love Worth Waiting: Hapily Ever After

Your Final Words:

You were created not just to fall in love — but to build eternity together. Your love story can be more than emotional — it can be eternal.

Now go — and make heaven at home.

A Love Worth Waiting: Hapily Ever After

Premarital Inventory

If you search Google for "Premarital Inventory by Focus on the Family," you will find an excellent resource designed to help couples prepare for marriage.

Bibliography

Research Reports, Surveys, and Organizational Studies

AACC. (2022). Marriage Recovery and Spiritual Intervention Study.

American Psychological Association. (2018). Understanding Teen Dating Violence. Retrieved from www.apa.org

American Psychological Association. (2019). Trauma & Marriage Study. Retrieved from www.apa.org

Barna Group. (2022a). Spiritual Vibrancy in the Home Study.

Barna Group. (2022b). State of the Church and Family Research.

Barna Group. (2022c). State of the Church and Marriage Resilience.

National Marriage Project. (2022). Before "I Do". University of Virginia.

Pew Research Center. (2021). Religion and Marriage Statistics in the U.S.

Harvard Human Flourishing Program. (2021). Prayer and Wellbeing Report.

Stanley, S. M. et al. (2006). Faith and Family During Crisis. National Marriage Project.

Stanley, S. M., Amato, P. R., Johnson, C. A., & Markman, H. J. (2006). Premarital Education, Relationship Quality, and Marital Stability. *Journal of Family Psychology, 20*(1), 117–126.

A Love Worth Waiting: Hapily Ever After

University of Notre Dame. (2021). Families and Faith Project.

Wilcox, W. B. (2017). The State of Our Unions. National Marriage Project.

Wilcox, W. B. (2020). The State of Our Unions. National Marriage Project.

Wilcox, W. B., & Wolfinger, N. H. (2019). Sex and Marriage in the 21st Century. Institute for Family Studies.

Peer-Reviewed Journal Articles

Busby, D. M., Carroll, J. S., & Willoughby, B. J. (2010). Compatibility or Restraint? The Effects of Sexual Timing on Marriage Relationships. *Journal of Sex Research, 47*(1), 29-38.

Joel, S., & MacDonald, G. (2013). I'm Just a Jealous Person: Sources of Jealousy in Romantic Relationships. *Personality and Social Psychology Bulletin, 39*(3), 393-404.

Books

Amen, D. (2015). *Change Your Brain, Change Your Life*. Harmony.

Balswick, J., & Balswick, J. (2006). *Authentic Human Sexuality: An Integrated Christian Approach*. IVP Academic.

Brother Lawrence. (1691). *The Practice of the Presence of God*.

Carnes, P. (2012). *The Betrayal Bond: Breaking Free of Exploitive Relationships*. Health Communications.

A Love Worth Waiting: Hapily Ever After

Chapman, G. (1992a). *The Five Love Languages*. Moody Publishers.

Chapman, G. (1992b). *The 5 Love Languages: The Secret to Love That Lasts*. Northfield Publishing.

Chapman, G. (1996). *Loving Your Spouse When You Feel Like Walking Away*. Moody Publishers.

Chapman, G. (2004a). *Hope for the Separated*. Moody Publishers.

Chapman, G. (2004b). *The Family You've Always Wanted*. Moody Publishers.

Cloud, H., & Townsend, J. (2000). *Boundaries in Dating*. Zondervan.

Dobson, J. (2002). *Love for a Lifetime*. Tyndale House Publishers.

Eggerichs, E. (2004). *Love and Respect*. Thomas Nelson.

Eldredge, J. (2016). *You and Me Forever*. Revell.

Eldredge, J., & Eldredge, S. (2016). *Love & War: Finding the Marriage You Dreamed Of*. WaterBrook.

Eldredge, J., & Stasi. (2005). *Captivating: Unveiling the Mystery of a Woman's Soul*. Thomas Nelson.

Gottman, J., & Silver, N. (2015). *The Seven Principles for Making Marriage Work*. Harmony Books. (Note: This title appears multiple times; one citation is sufficient.)

Haviland, J. (2014). *Exposing Soul Ties*. Destiny Image Publishers.

A Love Worth Waiting: Hapily Ever After

Johnson, S. (2008). *Hold Me Tight: Seven Conversations for a Lifetime of Love.* Little, Brown Spark.

Johnson, S. (2013). *Love Sense: The Revolutionary New Science of Romantic Relationships.* Little, Brown Spark.

Keller, T. (2011). *The Meaning of Marriage.* Penguin.

Laaser, M. (2009). *Healing the Wounds of Sexual Addiction.* Zondervan.

Levine, A., & Heller, R. (2010). *Attached: The New Science of Adult Attachment and How It Can Help You Find – and Keep – Love.* Tarcher Perigee.

Ortberg, J. (2018). *Eternity Is Now in Session.* Tyndale.

Parrott, L., & Parrott, L. (2015a). *Saving Your Marriage Before It Starts.* Zondervan.

Parrott, L., & Parrott, L. (2015b). *The Good Fight: How Conflict Can Bring You Closer.* Worthy Publishing.

Stormie Omartian. (2014). *The Power of a Praying Wife.* Harvest House Publishers.

T. Jakes, B. (2013). *Power for Parents and Partners: Building Spirit-Filled Homes.* Destiny Image.

Tish Harrison Warren. (2016). *Liturgy of the Ordinary: Sacred Practices in Everyday Life.* IVP Books.

Townsend, J. (2019). *People Fuel: Fill Your Tank for Life, Love, and Leadership.* Zondervan.

Townsend, J., & Cloud, H. (1992). *Boundaries.* Zondervan.

Townsend, J., & Cloud, H. (2000). *Boundaries in Dating.* Zondervan.

A Love Worth Waiting: Hapily Ever After

Trimm, C. (2013). *Commanding Your Morning*. Charisma House.

Trimm, C. (2014). *Prevail: Discover Your Strength in Hard Places*. Charisma House.

Valenzuela, Alfonso. (2005). *Youth in Love*. Living Ministry, INC.

Warren, T. H. (2016). *Liturgy of the Ordinary*. IVP.

Valenzuela, A. (1998). *Juventud enamorada*. [Libro fuera de publicación].

Valenzuela, A. (2005). *Youth in Love*. [Libro fuera de publicación].

Religious by Ellen G. White

White, E. G. (1898a). *The Desire of Ages*. Pacific Press Publishing.

White, E. G. (1898b). *The Desire of Ages*. Pacific Press.

White, E. G. (1905). *The Ministry of Healing*. Pacific Press.

White, E. G. (1930). *Messages to Young People*. Review & Herald.

White, E. G. (1952a). *Messages to Young People*. Review & Herald Publishing.

White, E. G. (1952b). *The Adventist Home*. Review & Herald Publishing Association.

White, E. G. (1980a). *The Adventist Home*. Review & Herald Publishing Association.

A Love Worth Waiting: Hapily Ever After

White, E. G. (1980b). *The Adventist Home*. Review & Herald.

White, E. G. (1990a). *Steps to Christ*. Review and Herald Publishing Association.

White, E. G. (1990b). *The Adventist Home*. Review and Herald Publishing Association.

White, E. G. (2002a). *Messages to Young People*. Pacific Press Publishing Association.

White, E. G. (2002b). *Steps to Christ*. Pacific Press Publishing Association.

White, E. G. (2002c). *The Adventist Home*. Pacific Press Publishing Association.

Wilson, J. (2020). *Together Again: Reconnecting with Your Spouse*. Lifeway.

Online Resources, Podcasts, and Web Articles

Biblestudyforyou.com. "30 Powerful Bible Verses About Unequally Yoked (Full Commentary)."

Free Bible Study Hub. (2024). "43 Scriptures on Dating and Courtship." Retrieved from FreeBibleStudyHub.com.

Gottman Institute. (2019). Small Things Often Podcast.

Serious Faith. (2009, September). What does it mean to be unequally yoked to the world? Retrieved from https://www.seriousfaith.com/2009/09/question-what-does-it-mean-to-be-unequally-yoked-to-the-world/

A Love Worth Waiting: Hapily Ever After

https://media.focusonthefamily.com/boundless/pdf/marriage-inventory.pdf

Biblical Texts and Classic Works

The Holy Bible, King James Version (KJV). Available at King James Bible Online.

The Holy Bible. (1611). King James Version.

www.ingramcontent.com/pod-product-compliance
Lightning Source LLC
Chambersburg PA
CBHW050627300426
44112CB00012B/1692